DEALERSHIP PROCESS SECRETS

Philip J. Cheatham

Central Desking House

CONTENTS

FREE AUDIOBOOK!

Listen to this book read by Philip J. Cheatham for FREE

@www.philipcheatham.com

Dedication

To Natasha, you are my sunrise in the middle of the pacific. This book and so much more wouldn't exist without your love and support.

WHY THIS BOOK?

This book is for Dealership Owners, Principles, COO's, CEO's, GM's and ALL top-level management in the dealership concerning your sales processes. This book is specifically about the processes in your Sales Department. You can flip to the U-Turn call chapter or any specific process chapter, to learn and implement just that process. I did my best to tell stories that will help you understand the "why" for each process. Your dealership Sales Department becomes a well-oiled machine once ALL of these processes are implemented. You can of course get ROI from each one of these processes individually. The goal of this book is to give you the ability to scale, monitor, and track your dealership's performance while having your finger on the pulse of your showroom floor from anywhere in the world with a quick glance at your desk-log. For this to be achieved, you will need to implement ALL of the Step-5 processes in section 2 and I highly advise that you also implement the 2 processes in section 1. While not mandatory, these processes will create even more organization for the crucial, and I would say mandatory, Step-5 processes. Giving you the ability to always ZERO in on exactly what areas are slipping before they inevitably slip. Resulting in less turnover, more sales and more profit. Your entire team will make more money and you will be happy to pay them. All of this resulting in happier customers. A confused mind always says "No." If your salespeople are confused, then they'll inevitably confuse your customers. Processes in your Sales Department are the solution for lower turnover and a high functioning staff. If people know what to do in your store, even if the processes are bad, you'll attract more talented candidates than if you're making it up as you go along. Your staff knowing what to do is directly related to your efficiency. When we don't know what to do, we hire somebody to tell us and this leaves us vulnerable and dependent. Your efficiency is directly related to your wallet. Your customers' experience is directly related to your sales team's happiness. Your salespersons' happiness is directly related to your sales team having direction.

This is why we are always talking about leadership. Leadership, however, isn't ever just a single person or multiple persons with an "ability to lead". Successful leadership starts with a structured organization first and then clear directions given to your leaders second. These directions turn into understood expectations that you set and must be met. Think about the military. Your leaders, just like those in the military should fall into place within the certain chain of command structure that you created, to your liking. Your leaders should be able to seamlessly integrate into your processes, follow, and direct them for you. You are vulnerable to consistent failure of your management team if you rely on them instead of your structured processes to "lead." Leaders need a structure for them to lead within and processes for them to follow and direct. The U.S. and the worlds' strongest known militaries have never relied on their leaders to "lead." Strong militaries rely solely on structure and processes that allow great leaders to lead. Structure and processes are how the worlds' greatest militaries create the worlds' greatest leaders. The better the structure and processes, the more organized and effective the military. Without the structure and processes first, you can't lead and you won't be able to find anybody that can. With structure and processes, you can pick your favorite promising green pea recruit, mold them to your liking and have them killing it on your sales desk in a matter of a couple years. The most loyal people you will ever create are the people you give the opportunity to lead and be effective in their leadership. John Maxwell defines leadership as your ability to create leaders. You can only create leaders with structure and processes. Leadership = processes.

Key sales processes are the solve to everything you ever wanted to happen inside your dealership. Just like growing a plant or building a home, you don't start with a ton of fertilizer or the roof first. I compiled 11 processes in this book that you could implement as you start hiring for a new dealership tomorrow. You will seamlessly grow at an exponential rate that will be beyond your own and your manufactures' expectations. You can also implement these processes into any store within 30 days. Some will be a lot easier than others.

Unfortunately, in some very poorly run dealerships, you will need to bring a hammer. Sometimes you will need a new face (your hammer) to come in and lay down the new laws. This is the only way to take a seriously underperforming store and turn it around. Sometimes you will lose people. Plain and simple, you didn't want these people. Their resistance to positive change will force them, once they leave your dealership, to make a shift in their lives. If you want a culture you can be proud of and a team you know will follow you to the end of the earth, you will understand sacrifices have to be made. If you really care about your team, you will give them the best structure and processes and remove any obstacles of bad attitudes surrounding them. If that means we lose some people, it's for the greater good.

How serious are you about lasting, positive change in your dealership's Sales Department? If this rubbed you the wrong way, I advise you to put down the book and go watch any Gordon Ramsey show. Whether you like his style or not, he proves in every episode, of every show he's ever made, that big changes and shifts occur when tough decisions are made quickly and stood behind. You must have conviction in these changes or you will never get them to stick. You cannot bend to anybody and let the people you care about down. You owe it to your team to tow the line. If the coach doesn't drill, the team doesn't win. The analogies are endless. Maybe your dealership is doing pretty well or great and you don't think you need a huge change, maybe just a little tune up. For you, I just ask that you read about each one of these processes and meditate on how you are doing things in your dealership

4

now. The stories I use should be entertaining. Think, contrast, and compare what you are doing now. If all you find are just a few gems of wisdom in the pages that follow, your time and money were well worth it. I do ask you to please consider implementing the entire gamut of processes in this book. The way it is written first, and then make your adjustments later. Do your best to implement the entirety of the processes laid out in this book. They do not need to be in order and you can implement the Step 5 Processes overnight using The Daily Desk available at www.centraldesking.com. You can then tune up your dealership even more by implementing the 2 processes in section 1 later.

◆ ◆ ◆

This book is also for GSM's, SM's, F+I Directors and ALL front-line management that want to have an impact. There are small pieces of gold hidden inside each of these chapters. Tiny little processes, we do consistently, like brushing our teeth, that solve so many problems while putting money in our pockets. The goal of this book is to understand what works best in auto dealerships on sales floors. Eliminating the headaches and increasing the amount of positive outcomes is always my goal. Having a finger on the pulse of your dealership, so that you can continue to grow even in a bad economy is what I have been able to successfully create the tools for; these tools work in any dealership. Our very first objective is a happy staff and a relentless dedication to our front-line salespeople. Have I lost you yet? The customer is second. If you have a happy marriage, you'll have happy kids. In this instance, if you have a happy platoon, you'll have success in battle. Business is battle. Since you have picked up this book, I think you would agree. The fitness of your people, your platoon, your team will always determine your success. The ability of your team to know what to do and when to do it is your power. Once again, think about the military's real power, it doesn't lie in individuals. It lies collectively in all of the individuals, individually within the organization, to know what to do and when to do it. Inside our industry today, we tend to throw people right onto the sales floor without any training, or very little. How do we then point the finger at our managers and blame them for "a lack of leadership?" Are you doing this right now? If you answered "yes," you know it's a copout while you are doing it. Today, we consistently give our front-line soldiers zero training and just throw them into battle and when they fail, then we blame our GSM, or our SM's, for "lack of leadership." If you go around talking to SM's today, they feel like they are in a catch 22 in this very common predicament across the board in our industry. Here lies opportunity for any dealer that wants to buck this bad idea and current trend. We are demanding our managers get better at "leadership" and we aren't giving them the tools to lead. All the great generals in history had trained soldiers. The same great generals would fail at training their soldiers during battle. Your soldiers cannot get in shape for battle during battle, that's a recipe for a massacre. This is the massacre we are seeing at all levels inside the dealership from entry level sales to the GM chair. This is the main reason for our industries massive turnover. It's the way we see it, not the way it is, which is the reason some dealers and groups have completely bucked this trend. They are using at least some of the secrets I will reveal inside this book.

My goal is that you take this book, read it in its entirety, and have fun with the stories. Then sit back, analyze what is happening in your dealership and realize that you have a massive amount of opportunity you can capitalize on by implementing these processes. I promise that if you read this book and either let Central Desking help you or do it all on your own, your ROI will be incalculable. If you are already implementing half of these processes, the other half will be a no brainer to you. First you need a desklog that your management and sales team will actually use. I suggest you don't waste any time and go to www.centraldesking.com and start your FREE trial for The Daily Desk.

ABOUT OUR BUSINESS

"There are 2,500 car dealerships in Los Angeles and I've only worked at 25 of them..."

-Shaun, 2014

T his is what Shaun, a salesman of mine would tell me when I first approached him to introduce myself as his new boss. A little less than 2 years later, I would hire him to work for me a second time at a different dealership. He really did have 13 W2's one year before I met him. As of now he had another year where he had 11 in-between working for me and hiring him again. Shaun is an older gentleman and a damn good salesman. He was consistently my #1 guy in the Internet Department I ran for a couple years. This isn't an uncommon tale in our business today. He hasn't had a drink in 50 years. If you ask him to do something, he does it. He was over twice my age and other than when I first approached him that day, I had virtually zero issues that I could point the blame in his direction for. He was a little rough but in a friendly, dry way. When he said that to me, I wasn't offended. I immediately laughed and asked, "Are there really 2,500 dealerships in Los Angeles?" He'd say, "I don't know" and from there we would go on to work great together. He'd later seek me out at a different dealership and of course I hired him. I think he lasted longer with me than he ever has anywhere else. Does that make me the most amazing manager? I doubt it. I know I've had managers that were much better at certain things than me. No, Shaun isn't special other than he's exactly who you want in your store selling your cars and handling your customers. Shaun also isn't special because he will quit bad management and a disorganized store within a month and keep doing it until he finds somewhere he can respect himself for staying. He also lives in Los Angeles with a ton of dealerships, you may be saying. You may be right. Shaun may have to stay in places that he knows lack organization in cities that have less opportunity. You also still don't get a happy Shaun. You don't get a fully productive Shaun like I did, and your customers don't get the Shaun experience mine did either. They get the frustrated either "I wish I could quit this place" Shaun, or the "I'm quitting soon, what do I care" Shaun. And when he doesn't care, he doesn't care. I got the "damn the car deals are falling from the sky here, he may be a young prick, but I love my manager Philip" Shaun. Most of the time. It wasn't always perfect, as with most top performers. We all know that already so that isn't the point of this story.

You are probably already gathering the main point. Your customer-facing-employees determine your customers' experience. It's true everywhere. Enthusiasm is contagious. Enthusiasm is also our best indicator of success.

"Sales is essentially a transfer of feelings."

-Zig Ziglar

If your people aren't feeling it, most likely, neither are your customers. Think about why you've left in the middle of a sales transaction and think about the times you stayed. It was all about the experience, specifically with your sales person. Our front-line sales team are the most important people inside our dealerships. Only once you became a GM did you realize they have a better job than you. Kidding, sort of. You know what I mean. However; our front-line sales team, our meet and greeters, and our test drivers are your face. When they look bad, so does the dealership to whomever is with them and so do you. We already know plopping a guy in front of a computer to watch some videos and then throwing him out on the sales floor makes no sense, even when we are doing it. Once we have processes in place, we never do this again.

I will give a detailed plan in Chapter 1 to execute the Product Specialist System, which will allow you to divide your training into 2 parts and make sure the people connecting with your customers aren't embarrassing you everyday. Maybe your people are sufficiently trained but unhappy; the processes I detail inside this book will morph your dealerships' culture into a positive environment you never thought possible. When Shaun comes to you, your dealership will have processes in place, that will allow Shaun to seamlessly integrate into your dealership and be a top performer for years to come. You will also attract the best candidates in your area for finance, closer and desk positions. You will be able to mold your green peas into your managers. You will be able to reasonably, fairly and effectively cut your pay plans and still pay a lot more because your volume and grosses will skyrocket. I've seen it over and over again. Today, I have been the main guy in our field making this positive evolution happen for dozens of dealerships along with the Central Desking Team. I have combined the most successful processes being used by the most successful dealerships that exist to give you a turnkey Sales Department that will crush every dealer surrounding your PMA and have them all complaining about you in 90 days or less. They'll all be talking about you, green with envy. With these processes, you will soon have all the best local talent and all of the happiest customers. And yes, haters.

I want you to know that you are probably already advertising enough, or a lot more than you need to or should. Once again, you will have to buck the trend of common thought and advice to go outside of common results. I urge you to look into exactly what the dealers you wonder about are doing to be successful. Look at their sales processes and ignore their advertisements for a minute, to investigate how the machine the customer enters actually works. If you are reading this then you've probably been to the Central Desking website. You can visit our website right now and have access to the Daily Desk within the next 5 minutes. I am sharing this with you for a point I will make shortly. We can do this at Central Desking because our product is simple; and we have tutorials you barely need to start using the entire system extremely effectively. The CRM companies can't really do this because their products are so complicated. One of these fancy CRM companies actually has a "Post Installation Transition Team" for when your staff isn't up and running after the 90 days it takes according to an Inside Sales Director. This particular Inside Sales Director told me, and I quote, "It takes 90 days to be up and running with our system." They obviously can't compete with Central Desking there, so you can't get access to one of these fancy CRMs within the next 10 minutes like you can with The Daily Desk. You can use our system starting today, effectively. It's easy and simple. You will have 14 days for free. You put in a credit card to avoid disruption of service, pick monthly or yearly and whether or not you want BirdEye (reputation managment) and within 5 minutes we will email you your account access. It's all setup for you to come into our process.

Now for my point: I know whose face you will see when coming into my realm. I know the process you will be led through and exactly what your experience will look like. Now we don't need a person there to greet you and the site is open 24 hours, 7 days a week, 365 days a year. My new sales guy, whom nobody trained, that we threw out on the floor because we got busy, will never greet you. See where I'm going with this?

You can get as many people to walk through your dealerships' doors as humanly possible. You can fill your showroom up past fire capacity. None of this will matter if the processes these customers land in when they arrive aren't setup to make deals happen.

<u>"Shouldn't we get better at managing the traffic we have before we bring in more?"</u>

-The savvy GM response to the "we need to advertise more" complaint.

On the internet they say, "you lose people with every click." Today in our industry, we are heavily focused on the internet. We should be, but we are forgetting about the people lost with every click inside our sales processes on our showroom floors. It's easier to keep them there in your showroom, yes. You are still losing people with every click in your sales process. It's the same as the internet. Your customer just has to make up a lie and leave instead of clicking out of a window. They are still clicking out.

Processes are the answer to every problem. Every problem occurs when somebody doesn't know what to do. When I was the GM at a Harley-Davidson Dealership, as you can imagine, bikes got dropped. The bike falling was never the problem. It was how it was handled afterwards. I would watch one of my Sales Managers flip out on the entire staff every time it happened. You know what happened? More bikes dropped on his watch than the rest of the managers combined. He made such a big deal out of it "what idiots," "what morons, they have no business moving these bikes." The Fit Specialists were so afraid to drop a bike when he was on duty, that they dropped a lot more bikes when he was on duty. Bikes will drop. How do we move on quickly and sell bikes even when "all the bikes are dropping?" Processes.

I will always give real advice, whether it sounds controversial or not. For example, you probably don't want to drug test your best salesperson if he just dropped a bike in your dealership, and you trust this person is an asset and not a liability on most days.

In California and some other states, it's illegal to fine your employees for accidentally damaging property or losing money unless its inside your pay-plan (speak to your own legal council). You still have to think of a process for when these type of events inevitably happen. I'm not going to recommend a process for bikes being dropped. You can hopefully figure out your own process. I never cared about this bullshit, our time is too limited. This is the same bullshit that takes your entire dealership "off market" too, so you need processes, but I really doubt you need to read a book to figure one out for dropped bikes.

Should you have free Fiji water or charge for water? I don't know. That's most likely answered by looking at your brand, your market, and asking the savvy person you have in charge of your dealerships' aesthetics, hopefully your marketing manager and your customers. You should also look at your local market. I know any advice concerning these questions across the board won't even work for all brands in all markets. To be honest, there are currently dealers running well-oiled machines out of trailers and tents. Machines that print money. There are also dealers with beautiful showrooms, free Fiji water and the cleanest Service Departments you've ever seen that have the manufacturer hoping and pushing for them to sell.

This book isn't about your receptionist smiling. This book will not list off a checklist of obvious nuances so that you can go clean the cobwebs off that 20-foot light you forgot about around back. For things like that, you are better off surveying or just picking up the phone and asking 25 of your customers than reading a book anyway. In my experience, your customer won't hold back on telling you that your bathroom is dirty, your sign is out, or that you need to cut your grass. Just ask them, they'll also tell you if your salespeople have bad breath and need deodorant, without fail every time, if you just start asking. That's the easiest way to find the red alerts, you don't need a book with a list. Your customers are the opposite of your friends that will never tell you that you have lettuce stuck in your teeth. They are the best people to ask. You will never ever, ever have a dealership up to the standard of every one of your customers. This will conclude the obviousness part of this book.

I didn't write this book just to write a book. I am also way too passionate about our buisness to actually complete something that is nothing but a bunch of obvious "clean your windows, don't use a blow up dinosaur" advice. I'd also bet there are still markets and brands where the blow up dinosaur still works phenomenally. The guy with the blow up dinosaur is eating everybody's lunch somewhere.

Some brands in certain markets benefit from a strong community presence and need a great reputation within their brands community to be successful. These dealers better pay close attention to their regulars that hang out in their dealerships. For other brands, in other markets, the crew that hangs out in your showroom on Saturday can actually be pests to your buying customers and to your business. Do your customers all talk to each other in forums online and in public at local events? If you're a Harley dealer, you bet they do, and you need to do things for your "hang out customers" at your Harley Dealership like Bike Nights. At a Lexus dealership, you probably won't create much loyalty among a customer base that isn't a community on their own by gathering them together and feeding them. They will most likely still go to your competitor over $5 in payment when they are looking for their next car and forget all about your free food they ate if that was already their behavior. You need a community of your customers to create loyalty with gatherings. This is why Lexus has Lexus Club. Lexus Club was, and is, an attempt at gathering a community around the brand outside the actual dealerships. Needless to say, Lexus Club is a very small subset of Lexus customers and not very successful in its attempt, unlike

H.O.G. has been for Harley-Davidson. I'm not saying don't try, if you are Lexus Dealer, to create whatever you want. I am pointing out that with each brand and market, you have different opportunities to capitalize on, and that certain things that provide massive ROI for one brand in one market may provide nothing to another brand in another market. Not having bad breath, knowing whether or not your customers have an outside community together or respond to the blow up dinosaur and hot dog Sundays should be common sense. All of this varies greatly across different brands and markets. You should know your customer and your market and not try to reinvent the wheel. This is not what this book is about.

This book is about pro secrets of the best operators concerning your sales processes. This book is about keeping your substance addicted salesperson at work and out of trouble, making money for you, year after year. Controversial statement? Sure. I'd also say its humanitarian. Our business is an amazing place for people with idle hands to be productive in our society and economy that otherwise would be out hurting themselves or others. I'm just being honest and I think this is a wonderful thing. Our business has saved a lot of people from lives of destruction, including me.

This book is about actual needle moving processes that your customer will appreciate but couldn't explain to you. These processes will explode your unit sales and improve your gross dramatically. Either way, whether it actually be related to your dealerships' success or an everyday bullshit house cleaning problem you have inside your dealership, it can be solved by a process.

INTRODUCTION

"He was talking about opening cans of worms and not stepping in bear traps the entire week; by the time we were done I thought I was going hunting, not selling cars..."

-Anonymous, 2004

Ahmed: "Oh fuck, it's Mrs. Henderson, holy shit buddy, watt dee fuck? God damnit! Now I gotta throw out a perfectly good dip, maybe I can save it, oh fuck it (Ahmed spits out his dip in the sales office trash can), this lady is such a fucking cunt, Jay."

Ahmed walks out of the sales office.

Jay: "Have fun!"

Ahmed: "Mrs. Henderson, oh my! What a pleasure! So nice to see you! So happy you stopped by, to see me... I'm sure?"

Mrs. Henderson: "Ahmed, we are not happy at all, where is that short, fat lying mother fucker named Leonard Brown?"

Ahmed: "Lenny? What did Lenny lie about? Maybe I can help Mrs. Henderson..."

Mrs. Henderson: "Where is he?"

Ahmed: "Ok, Mrs. Henderson let me see if I can find him for you, have a seat over here, I will go look for him for you, I will be right back."

Ahmed walks back into the sales office.

Ahmed: (laughing voice) "Oh fuck, this lady wants to kill Lenny, call down to him and tell him to go hide, Jay."

Jay: (thick Texas accent) "What does she want?"

Ahmed: (heavy laughing voice) "I got no idea she called Lenny a "short, fat lying mother fucker, Jay."

Jay: "Yeah I heard that part."

Jay dials Lenny's extension on speaker.

Jay: "Lenny what did you do to this lady up here calling you a short, fat lying mother fucker?".

Lenny: "Who, Jay?"

Jay: "What's her name, Ahmed?"

Ahmed: (speaks into Jay's phone) "It's Mrs. Henderson, Lenny, and she wants your ass!"

All we heard was a click.

Jay: "Lenny? Lenny?, Ahmed, go back there and see what the fuck's wrong with Lenny, who's her 'prod'?" (short for Product Specialist).

Ahmed: "I think it's Henry Jay, look it up in the deal!"

Jay: "Yeah, it's Henry."

Jay pages Henry to the sales desk.

Jay: "Henry, sales desk."

Henry: "Yes, Jay."

Jay: "Henry, do you know what's wrong with your customer? Why's she wanna slit Lenny's throat?"

Henry: "Oh yeah, she called me yesterday and said she was coming in to talk to him and that he sold her chrome wheels for $3,000. I told her I thought that's what we charged. She said, that's not what Lenny told her, so I just told her to come in" (shrugs shoulders).

Jay: "Alright, go sit with her and calm her down while I figure out what happened, more goddamn shit, Barry! More shit!" (Barry was the other Sales Manager)

Jay leaves to go find Lenny and meets Ahmed in the back near his office.

Ahmed: "I can't find him, Jay. I even looked in the bathroom, he isn't here."

Jay: "What the fuck is going on? He doesn't even have a cell phone, he needs to get a cell phone!"

Ahmed: "Well he's usually in his office."

Jay: "Let me go talk to this lady."

Jay walks back up to the customer lounge where Mrs. Henderson is sitting.

Jay: "Hello, Mrs. Henderson, is it?"

Mrs. Henderson: "Yes."

Jay: "Hello, I'm Jay. I'm the General Sales Manager, I understand there's an issue..."

Mrs. Henderson: "Yes, I don't have a problem with anybody here except that short, fat lying mother fucker named Leonard Brown!"

Jay: "What did Lenny do?"

Mrs. Henderson: "He's a liar! He told me and my husband the chromes were $90 a month and I got home and showed my mother and she showed me he charged me $2,995 dollars and taxes! So I already took the chrome wheels off the car. The car is at home with no wheels and my boys are outside, they are here to give the wheels back. So, I am just going to sit right here and wait until I get my $2,995 plus sales tax back and we can trade the wheels back please Mr. Jay..."

Jay looks outside and sees Mrs. Henderson's 3 sons that look like they are ready to start something, they also had the wheels stacked up in front of their car in customer parking.

Ahmed waves Jay over.

Ahmed: "Lenny is hiding in the Service Department bathroom."

Jay: "What the hell is he doing back there?"

Ahmed: "He thinks her sons are going to kick his ass and I

think he's right Jay, look at them out there waiting."

Jay: "Fuck I don't need this shit."

Jay goes back into the sales office and calls over to accounting.

Jay: "Fuck this..." "Hey Emily...deal number 169874, I need a $2,995 check plus the sales tax quickly please, I'll come get it in 5 minutes."

Jay walks back out to Mrs. Henderson.

Jay: "Mrs. Henderson, I have a check coming for $2,995 plus your sales tax coming over in the next 5 minutes. I'm going to hand it to you, you can keep the wheels and your payments won't change. Can your sons handle putting your wheels back on since the car isn't here?"

Mrs. Henderson: "Oh Mr. Jay, yes my boys took them off, they can put them back on for me, thank you so much Mr. Jay, so you are getting me a check right now?"

Jay: "Yes."

Mrs. Henderson: "Oh Mr. Jay I have to come back and thank you, let me go tell my sons."

Jay: "Ok Mrs. Henderson."

We would all laugh and call Lenny "that short, fat lying mother fucker named Leonard Brown" for the next decade.

I was standing in the sales office when this all took place. It was my 3rd month in the car business and my first month in finance. Lenny had just been promoted to Finance Director a month before and had chosen me from the 24 Product Specialist's to be a Finance Manager. Lenny had put up a fight for me too; it was solely his idea to pick me when he was promoted to Finance Director. The owner didn't even really know who I was. I was just another one of dozens of Product Specialists that had come to him in the past 2 and a half years and had a couple good starting months. Maybe Lenny had noticed me living at the dealership and could tell inside my head that I would constantly say to myself, "They'd have to call the police to get me out of here or fire me." Maybe it was just like he would tell me later "You have a trusting face, that's why I picked you." I think it was a combination today.

The year prior to getting hired here, only a few months before, had been the most difficult year of my life. I had moved to Florida from California where I had been working as a cook at The Ritz Carlton to go back to school. I had done well in the culinary world from 18-20 years old. I had been told by The Ritz Carlton, who is still owned by Marriott, that if I went to culinary school, I would get a chef position. Not the executive chef role, but a chef role. You have to have a culinary degree similar to an officer in the military in Marriott to hold any chef role. Under the chefs were the cooks I-IV. I had started as a cook IV and now was a cook I. This chef role was promising, as people who had gone to culinary school were not guaranteed chef roles, you just needed a culinary degree to hold a chef role. I watched plenty of people come and go who had been to culinary school while I worked at The Ritz. Without experience, culinary school just meant you started as a cook IV like I did and for some it meant you would quit your first week after going to school.

There were only 2 schools I wanted to go to, and one was $45,000 and the other was $55,000. I did the math and it didn't make a lot of sense to me. I had loved working in the kitchen, being given more opportunities, and learning. Without this experience I wouldn't have been prepared for the car business. I learned work ethic in a very fast paced, difficult environment;

the professional kitchen. I cherish this life experience now. I can cook anything I want at home and blow people away now, which is awesome. What I really gained from this experience that would matter to my next career path though, was an understanding of personal responsibility and work ethic.

I would move to Orlando after convincing my mom to let me move in with her after she had just moved to Florida from Northern Virginia. The plan was to go back to school. I would get there and out of state tuition would be significantly more than in state tuition. I then changed my plan to work and take a few courses as I could afford them each semester until I became a Florida resident, and load up at a much smaller tuition. My first job applications would be to fine dining restaurants and hotels. I was consistently told that $8 an hour would be my rate. I was making $14.50 an hour when I left The Ritz Carlton in California, which looking back, was pretty good money for a 20-year-old in 2003. I would always have around 10 overtime hours, too.

I would end up going around the entire City of Orlando filling out applications for every car dealership in the city. I had bought my first car on my own as soon as I started making a little money back in California. I had even flirted with the idea of selling cars back there and was hired the same day at a non luxury brand dealership and at The Ritz Carlton. My mom had convinced me to pick The Ritz Carlton saying "That's a shark-eat-shark business" and "Don't do commission only!" I'm glad I didn't do it back then, I didn't need that much money and the restaurant business would turn out to be a great preparation for the car business.

Trying to get a job again in Florida at a dealership would prove to be impossible. After applying to literally every franchise dealership in the city, I was interviewed a few times in offices, and more times in showrooms, and even more times on the side of the dealership, not knowing what a GSM even was back then, or who to ask for. I would even take a couple personality tests and be told once "these are the worst results I've ever seen, stop trying to work in this business, these results say you'll never make it." My Mom and my sister would tell me the same thing. I would finally get hired at a non-luxury brand store in a class of about 25 people. A week into the training, the class would be down to 15 or so and after we all went to do our drug test at the same location, we'd lose another 5, with one actually getting caught with a bag of pee. A few days later when there were about 6 of us left, I was pulled out and told "You are my most promising guy, but they say upstairs that you can't work here unless you clear up some tickets you have in California." I was dead broke, and this wasn't happening.

I would end up getting a job valet parking for a few months until they fired me. My mom kicked me out and told me I couldn't live in her house and needed to get a secure job. My mom and sister both told me "you need to go flip burgers." I was going to school, but only to a few classes. I had a 4.0 GPA at the time. I also had no money and wasn't able to pay my electric bill or my car payment on my Lexus. I was shaving with a candle in the morning to go to a job where we would knock door-to-door for a political candidate. I was hiding my car 3 apartment complexes away because Lexus Financial was actively looking for it as I was now over 120 days late.

I stayed up late one night and really thought about what I wanted to do. I had felt banished from even being allowed to do car sales. I decided I would go into the academic arena that night. I have been in love with learning since shortly after leaving high school; I hated learning until I was out of school. I loved community college. I would give back and become a professor, I decided.

I would wake up the next day, light some candles in the bathroom to shave, and get ready to go to work. I noticed a voicemail on my flip phone I had back then, and called to listen. "This is Fred with New Car Luxury Dealership, I am calling because I have your application here and if you are still interested in working here, call me back, bye." I remembered what I had decided the previous night for literally a split second as I started to get really excited and happy. I called him back immediately. I had to leave a voicemail and wait until he called me back. When he called me back, he asked me if I could come in and interview that coming Monday. I said yes, even though I had work. I hung up and jumped over my couch a few times while screaming like a 4-year-old girl. It didn't take a millisecond for me to forget all about everything I had planned the night before. Fuck all this candle and hiding my car shit, I'm going to make money!

I would call in sick to my door-to door job and go to the interview on Monday. Fred would sit there and explain the job to me. "You don't do the numbers, you aren't allowed to talk about the numbers." He'd ask me some questions about why I wanted to work there etc., and then he'd ask, "can you pass a drug test and sell 10 cars?" I couldn't believe I was actually getting hired at a Luxury Dealership after trying so hard with no results. I said, "y-y-y-y-y-y-yes". He said, "Ok come back next week, same time, you will be in a class with some other guys and go take this form to this address and pee in a cup now, I will call you on Friday to remind you to wear black dress shoes, black pants, and a white polo."

I had filled out the application for this job 11 months earlier. It was one of the first applications I had filled out. I was so ecstatic. I would run and tell my mom, who was very skeptical and would tell me "If you don't make any money in your first month, I'd get out of there and all my friends say the same thing." Nobody I knew thought I was going to make it or gave me any words of encouragement, just questions concerning my readiness for this industry.

I'm going to tell you something and warn you up front because it offends some people. One of my later Finance Directors would jokingly say, "That's the sickest thing that I've ever heard," when I would tell him and then he'd ask me to retell it to people; "tell him, tell him what you told me about when you were little," chuckling as if I was some weird science experiment.

First, I have to tell you my sister and I grew up very privileged. For a moment at least. We went on vacations. We went to all the museums and all the historical sites in the Washington D.C. area as children. From The White House to Gettysburg and Williamsburg, even private tours on the old coal train that runs under D.C. to all the buildings that only government and all the congressman and senators use. My mom actually dated Ted Kennedy and he would bring me Macy's bags of candy when I was 7. We went to Montessori schools. We grew up very, very well. We would have to fend for ourselves as adults later on, but we grew up very privileged. I have no idea how many times I actually went to the Kennedy Center before I was 12-years-old. We even have our kid sized hand imprints on the wall of the Holocaust Museum because of our parents' donations. Our parents were real players in the DC arena in the 80's and we would still live very well throughout the 90's. Both of our parents also had well-to-do parents. They would get divorced when I was 6 and my Dad would move to Tennessee then Texas, but there was a time when they were both very well connected and doing very well in the DC area. My sister and I were both very young and by the time we became adults, let's just say this changed quite a bit.

I would go to the BMW dealership with my mom when I was around 4, to buy her cars and I would also go with her when she got them serviced. I thought the car dealership was the coolest place I had ever been to in the entire world, and like I said I had a very spoiled upbringing. The car dealership was my Disneyland. I thought it was spectacular at 4 years old. I remember thinking this before my head was as high as the pool table in the employee lounge that my mom's college friend, who was her salesman, would let me hang out in. I remember the vending machines in there like it was yesterday. I would pretend I worked there at 4 years old, I thought it was so cool. I wanted to be her salesman when we would go on test drives and thought "his job is to drive the cars all day." "This is the coolest job ever," I thought. I was 4 and to this day I feel the same way. I imagine I would've voiced this to my mom very early and she would probably tell me something like "you'll never have to do that." I can't come up with another reason I never thought I would end up working in a dealership growing up. "If everything were ever to go completely wrong and I needed a job, 'I'd get to work at a dealership,' not 'I'd have to work at a dealership." This was how my mind, that had yet to ever know financial struggles, thought. I never thought that I would ever work in a dealership growing up, even though I thought it was the coolest place you could ever work. I was always attracted to the mysteriousness. I had no idea how soon I'd actually be that guy in the sales tower that "knows all the secrets." I still thought it was the coolest place you could go at 21-years-old. I still do today. It's where I drive my brand new cars off the lot. I think I understand this specialness in just an extra special way. I love it.

I was finally in again, but still worried about the haunting driving record in California. This dealership, I guess, would never run my California driving record. The DMVs would link up nationally a couple years later and Florida would suspend my license for my California tickets. Even though it would sting, I was making money and was able to pay California around $3,000 to clean up these tickets I had left unpaid for years. Thank you, car business!

I'd arrive at the dealership the following Monday after passing my drug and background check, I was told. I was of course still frightened about the California tickets, but I was going to try anyway. I'd get to the dealership around an hour early and just drive around the area for a little while before going in about a half hour early. I was the first one there and another 3 guys would show up. Fred would come and take us to a training room and teach us

26

everyday for an entire week.

This was the coolest week of my entire life up until this point. My car was still in repossession status with Lexus Financial and my lights were still off, but I would sit out on my patio reading the 2004 and 2005 new luxury car brochures all night and go back to the dealership the next day, wishing I could go in earlier and stay longer. As broke as I was, this was a very special time for me. I did not take this opportunity lightly. I decided to go all in. I didn't care at all about having a social life.

Fred told us "you can come into this business with a nickel in your pocket and quickly have a new car, a nice place, and some money to spend." I just wanted to turn my lights back on and send 5 back payments to Lexus Financial. Fred was truly in love with the luxury product we were selling. He loved what he did too and was great with the customers. He was a perfect fit for Training Director. He spoke in a ton of analogies and would constantly say "you don't want to open a can worms" or "step in a bear trap" as he would give us examples of things that could happen if we didn't follow the processes he was teaching us. I loved it. I ate it up. Every last thing Fred said.

He taught us about the product and would give us homework assignments. I didn't even have a TV I could turn on, so I over studied and over learned everything. He would also teach us about people and one great example I would go on to teach for the next 15 years would be, "follow me." He told us "when you tell people, 'follow me', they will just follow you... until... you look back, you can't look back. But you can say, 'follow me' and walk around the building 3 times, turn around, and they will be there. You all do it too when somebody says, 'follow me', you just do, people are like dogs. Try it, it works!" It does. I couldn't wait to try it. Doing that was the first time I felt like a pro in the business. I could just get people to follow me around at my command, how cool! I knew I'd love this business; I would tell my mom.

He taught us all of our duties from A-Z. Our pay plan and how to work it properly. The main duties of a Product Specialist, that I will detail in the first chapter of this book, which goes over this process in extreme detail. This dealership I worked in had it down to a science. I still have yet to come across a dealership with the Product Specialist System more dialed in and I've been around quite a bit demoing The Daily Desk. I was very fortunate to start my career where I did.

Fred taught us what we would do when coming in first thing in the morning after putting our names on the list. We had a list that went in order, they still do. He taught us how to test drive and to assume instead of asking, and how to do that properly. "Don't ask 'do you want to drive?,' say 'I'll go get the keys." He taught us how to fill out the guest card properly so that "the desk doesn't throw it back at you;" and he would teach us to only say "I have a deal" in the sales office.

He told us that when we finish filling out our guest card, hand it into the sales desk, only after completing a test-drive. (This store drives 99% of the people that come onto their lot.) We were to walk into the sales desk, put our guest card on the counter and say, "I have a deal!" and get the fuck out of the sales office. "Don't say anything else!" He drilled down on this and said it was very important and that "they will rip your head off if you don't do this." So, say it with me, "I have a deal,' I'm serious." He told us that everyday of the training.

The best part of the training, of course, was actually driving the cars. I couldn't wait to own a much newer car than I had myself. My favorite one at the time was the convertible. I remember looking at it when we got one valeted at my valet job that I was fired from. The valet director saw me and said, "why are you looking at that car? You'll never afford that." I was driving it now though, down the actual street, and for work! I would later have the same valet director that told me that, still working there 2 years later, valet my car, the same convertible, true story. That would be the sweetest moment of my life up until that point. Thank God I got fired, but I was actually parked when a 7 or 8 year employee crashed into me, and that's why I got fired. Thank you, both!

I couldn't wait to actually start selling and was praying every night that nothing would happen like it did at the non-luxury car store with my driving record. Fred told us on the last day in the training room to come back the next day wearing shirts that he would give us, making it official, and that we would "shadow" a Product Specialist and learn from them tomorrow, on Saturday, and would "go live" on Monday after taking Sunday off.

I came in the next day an hour early at least. I was put with Jenny, who had been in the store before the Product Specialist System, but had been a Product Specialist now for two years. Jenny had been at the store for 9 years. I couldn't believe that. I was 12 when she started working there. I certainly had no idea I would actually work at this same dealership 10 years later. I thought that was an eternity. Here I was learning from Jenny. I would do 3 or 4 test drives with Jenny that day and watch everything she did. She sold 1 car and I couldn't wait to do it myself.

I'd come back Monday and get my first opportunity. I was 2nd on the list my first day. I couldn't believe it. I had come an hour early to be first on the list. I would take the second up of the day and follow exactly what I had been told. It all worked. "Follow me", "I'll be right back with the keys, and we'll drive her." It was amazing. You'd think I had been doing this for years.

Here I was, writing up my first guest card ever. My customers loved me and seemed like they were ready to buy the car, other than that he kept telling me, "If they show me less than 10K for my trade, I'm leaving, kid." He kept saying it over and over. His wife even said, "he will too."

Now I had a problem. I had no idea what to do and I couldn't find Fred anywhere. I knew I was supposed to just say "I have a deal," but this customer was also telling me he was going to leave if we didn't give him 10k for his trade. I was stuck between "should I let them know he's going to leave" or do the "I have a deal" thing. I really didn't know what to do. I decided they definitely want to know this information; this has got to be an exception. Ok I'll go tell them. I walk into the sales office. I've been introduced to the 2 guys sitting behind the sales desk that you have to walk up a couple stairs to get behind only once, and with the other 3 guys in my training class. I didn't know them at all yet. I still know them both today.

I walk up and I drop my guest card on the countertop in front of them and proceed to tell them, "my customer says he is going to leave if we don't give him 10k for his trade-in, he says he won't..." I get cut off, "stop right there son, just stop talking." The both of them had been looking at me with a glare like I had just stood up at their Thanksgiving dinner and started getting naked. Time slowed down as far as it could. I shut up quickly when he let me. He picked up the phone and over the pager said, "Fred, sales desk," in his thick Texas accent. Fred comes flying into the sales office like Kramer used to on Seinfeld. "What Jay? What Jay?" Jay says, "what the fuck, Fred can you get these guys to say 4 simple fucking words 'I have a deal.' Is it that fucking difficult? What the fuck do you do back there with these ingrates for a full fucking week?" Fred turns and looks at me and I stop before he can say anything and say, "I get it. Yes, Fred told us. Sorry I thought you'd..." "Son, I probably don't want to know anything you think I do," Jay interrupts. "Yes sir, 'I have a deal.' It'll never happen again, Jay". "Good. Fuck, Fred, get the fuck out of my office." I jumped in front of Fred to get the fuck out before he could get the fuck out and went and sat back down with my customers.

As you can imagine, I was devastated. I thought I had really messed up. I thought I had really let down Fred too, I apologized to Fred and he just said, "I told you, just don't ever do that one again." I stayed up all night thinking I really screwed up bad and that they'd never forget it. I don't think I'd ever even hear about it ever again. I doubt Jay or Fred even remembers this today, because I'd certainly never remind them. Life moved fast in this dealership. This was another thing I'd love about the business. We could be wanting to kill each other today and eating lunch together tomorrow. Jay doesn't remember half the things he almost fired me over today and doesn't even remember firing me once, until I reminded him. Then he asked, "why did I do that?" He fired a lot of people, and some multiple times. He fired one person 11 times and another person 9 times. He only fired me once and hired me back the next day.

I, however, took the experience very seriously. I didn't understand the "I have a deal" process at all. Most people probably never cared and just did it for years. I had to understand it, but I wasn't going to question it now. That night I told myself after not being able to figure it out and I certainly didn't want to ever go ask why, that I would just do whatever they told me to do, after all I wanted to be successful in this business so badly. They probably knew something I didn't. I decided if they asked me to do something, that I would just do it and not ask any questions or worry about why and assume they knew better than me. This was probably the best attitude and is the best attitude you can enter the car business with. This little decision of mine, thanks to my "I have a deal" blunder right out of the gate on my very first write-up, allowed me to propel very quickly. I became great at learning by just following and not asking and thinking about it later, by myself. This was also definitely an important prerequisite to my finance promotion, after only selling cars for 2 months at 21-years-old.

I'd go on to sell 12 cars my first month and 17 my second. I was able to get my lights turned on and get current on everything except my car with my first month's check. Halfway through my second month, I was told that the Finance Director wanted to speak with me. Now there had been a different guy at the desk with Jay when I started a month ago. He had worked there for 9 years and was fired my first month in the dealership. They promoted the Finance Director Barry to the desk and had promoted Lenny to Finance Director. I had no idea why he wanted to speak to me, but I went back to see him. He sat me down and asked me some questions and then asked, "do you know what we do back here?" I said, "no, not really." He explained they do the paperwork and it's a lot of work but they make money from selling too. He knew I was worried about becoming some sort of a paper pusher I think, and that is exactly what was going through my head. I had only been selling for 2 months and I was in heaven with what I was already doing. I had no clue what this opportunity really meant at the time, and I wouldn't really understand what a break this would actually be for me and my career for years to come. Lenny told me from what he had seen, that he thought I was a great fit and that he wanted me to start the following month. He also wanted me to think about it and talk to him in 2 days. He also told me that if I said yes, I would still also have to interview with Nathan, the owner.

I probably would've sold 25 cars my second month and not 17 had this not happened. I didn't know what to do. Half the dealership wanted to take me out, buy me a drink and give me advice. Some people told me I was crazy if I didn't do it, best advice being "that's how you get on the desk." Other people would tell me I was crazy if I did it, and that it was some sort of trap to stop me from doing what I was already doing so well at, including Fred who I now know just didn't want to lose me from sales. I didn't know who to believe, I really didn't. I'd go talk it out with my mom, who was now all of a sudden so proud of me, after telling me only a couple months earlier to quit. She would hate it for the next 14 years everytime I would bring that up. She, however, was the one that would convince me to take the leap and go for the promotion after a very long talk. Two people, not even knowing what they were talking about. You may think this was an obvious decision, it wasn't. I had worked at one dealership and didn't know anybody inside the industry. If it wasn't for my mom, who also had no idea what a Finance Manager does, I wouldn't have done it. She convinced me I had nothing to lose and that they must see something in me, so I did it.

Lenny had really stuck his neck out for me to get in. I was the most serious person working there at the time. My entire first month, I had an apartment without lights so I stayed at the dealership as long as I could. I was ecstatic when I was told I was allowed to work on my days off. The first day I took off would be after about 3 weeks; that's all my 21-year-old body and mind could take, and I had to stay home and sleep for a day. The owner thought Lenny was nuts, but let him hire me anyway. I had one tie I wore everyday for my first month. It was embarrassing but I didn't care at all. I would have a collection of over 100 by the same time the following year.

The other 3 guys in my training class would last a week, 8 weeks and 12 weeks. One I would never hear from again. One, I would go to his first wedding. I missed his last, apparently. The other I still saw before he would die only a few years later at 28 in a horrible car accident.

I would still work at this Dealership in 2014 before moving to California to start at another luxury car dealership. I had gotten the job from Florida.

The training at this dealership is still pretty serious. The dealership yielded only me as a profitable result from this particular training and much less from many others. The quote at the top of this introduction is from the guy that lasted 12 weeks whose first wedding I would attend with my now wife. The training meant nothing to him as he thought he was "going hunting," he would say. Without this training for me however and the Product Specialist System, I doubt I would work in our beloved business. I definitely wouldn't have excelled as quickly as I did and been able to continue having success at every position without this experience the way it was. I wasn't ready. My mom was actually right. I never did get to explain the mystery to her, she just thought she was wrong. I had just happened to be in the wrong place at the right time. This would of course also only be the first time.

Section 1: Setup Processes

THE PRODUCT SPECIALIST

(Laying the Foundation)

"*I was in Europe on Big Business when I came up with this whole Product Specialist System.*"

-Anthony Rocco, 2004

"I was in Europe on Big Business when I came up with this Product Specialist idea," this is me talking to a customer just shooting the shit. They were asking me where I was because I was gone for the past 2 months. My name is Anthony Rocco, really, I was in jail after another Sales Manager called my parole officer to tell her I left the dealership. I wasn't supposed to do that on work release, but I just went across the street to the ABC store to get a cigar. These guys don't want me around because they're lazy and sleep all day. I wouldn't even know this manager did this to me for over a decade, but the rest of the dealership knew. Anyway, that's another story for another day. I had this new Product Specialist kid with my customers, named Phil Cheatham. They had bought 3 or 4 cars from me and they were asking me about this new system I came up with just a couple years back. You see, I'm a closer, I shouldn't even be in this business, but I got in some trouble and lost my insurance practice. I can close anybody on anything though, I even closed the owner on letting me work here because of how well I did my first month before my background check came back. I sold 20 cars my first month, what were they going to do, fire me? They almost did! Can you believe that? I talked him into letting me stay, I mean how can you fire me? Nobody else can put up these numbers.

So these folks are asking me about how this whole Product Specialist thing works and where I was when I came up with it, so instead of telling them I was in jail, I'd tell them about how I invented the whole thing while I was in Europe on some unavoidable "Big Business."

Anthony: "So, I was in Europe on some Big Business, I was eating lunch and I started really thinking about the problems we have in our industry. You know some of these guys just don't know how to handle customers, they aren't willing to go the extra distance for you guys, I live for you guys, you guys know that. So, I'm pondering these issues in Europe. You know running a car dealership these days is tough work! It was the last time I was in Europe just eating lunch, when all hell broke loose here, oh yeah! These guys couldn't do it without me while I was gone. There's another guy here that sleeps all day with his feet in a trashcan, can you believe that? Ok, what did you guys want to pay for this car again? Are we leasing? Let me go run the numbers for you."

Customer: "Um, we don't want to lease."

Anthony: "What do you mean you're not leasing? Are you nuts? Hold on ok, I'll be right back with your purchase numbers and I'll show you a lease, you guys will be really smart to lease. Anyway, we will figure it out. What car are we trying to put you guys in again folks? Does that one have 4 cylinders or 6? (laughs) Would you believe I don't even know?"

Anthony Slows down for just a second, puts his hand on his waist, lowers his glasses, and looks the customers right in their eyes...

Anthony: "I just sell 'em! That's what we need Philip for! Alright, gonna get you guys all set. I'll be right back."

Customer: "It's amazing how he runs the store all the way from Europe, I bet he's a great boss!"

Me: "Yeah it is and yes, yes he is."

I didn't quite understand Anthony's responsibilities yet myself, and had no idea whether anything he was saying was true or not, I assumed it all was.

Anthony: "Alright I'm back, you guys are gonna love what I put together for you, wait wait... hold on, no that's not for you. Oh yeah, how long did you guys want to lease?"

Customer: "Honey do you want to lease?"

Customer's Husband: "No, we are not leasing."

Anthony: "Don't be silly guys, all my customers lease, you gotta trust me on this, I'll be right back."

Customer: "He knows what he's doing honey, I trust him... are you in school while you do this job Philip?"

Me: "No, we work full time, I was..."

Customer: "Oh no, you have to go to school, make sure you at least get the piece of paper."

Me: "Ok I will."

Anthony runs up, papers in both hands and a little erratic. He throws one down on the table and starts reading it.

Anthony: "No, not this one. Oh my god I gotta do everything, these guys are clueless (talking to himself)." "Oh ok, here it is..."

Anthony throws all the other papers on the floor like nothing matters but this customer's numbers and paper. He places his glasses an inch lower on his nose so he can see over them and looks down right into the customer's eyes and says:

Anthony: "I'm sorry guys they got me doing everything around here. Ok, let's put you guys in a 24 month lease right now. I'm really not supposed to tell you this, but the bank had a residual error, house loses... plus I can get you guys out 6 months early, you just pay $703 a month."

Customer: "$703 a month? For a lease! We were hoping to get to $500 on another purchase."

Anthony: "Yeah with 25K down! You only have to put down $7,500 on this lease program you aren't even supposed to know about, and you're only in the car for a year! I get all my customers out early; this is how you buy a car these days, folks! I do this for a living! This is how I'm doing it with all my high-end clientele. Hold on I'll be right back, I just thought of something."

Anthony comes back with an erratic energy about 10 minutes later after leaving the customers waiting.

Anthony: "Hey ok I'm back, what do you guys need? Shit, oh yeah I got it all figured out. They are pissed at me and sorry for the language and chaotic day... look I told them you are my best customers and really sweet people. So oh yeah, here, I almost forgot, sign here (now he pulls their paper from a bunch of other papers and acts like theirs is unimportant). I got you guys right under $700 a month on a 29 month lease and I'll get you guys out in a year, just don't tell your neighbors and keep that our secret, ok? You know I should take this deal for my daughter. She needs a new car and loves these."

Customer: "Yes."

Anthony puts the pen in the husband's hand.

Anthony: "You just have to pay $7,500 plus drives so it's eleven thousand four hundred something dollars. You guys don't care about the nickels, alright Philip, right? Philip go get these lovely folks their car gassed up, come on hurry up! Their time is money! I'm going to take you guys over to the customer lounge. Follow me while finance gets ready for you. Good seeing you folks."

Anthony runs into the sales office and says "another one" as he places his signed deal on the desk.

That was Anthony Rocco and while he never told these customers the story of how he invented the Product Specialist System, he would tell me. I use to pick him up in the morning from work release and drop him off too, he told me a lot during those car rides. He was in jail, not in Europe when he came up with it. He was responsible for half of the dealership's monthly sales when he wasn't in jail. He was also right that he just couldn't teach anybody how to be Anthony Rocco. Anthony was a master. I once watched him respond to a customer by saying, "Your dad told you never to lease? Who are you going to believe, me or your dad?" Followed by his famous "I do this for a living." The deal came into my finance office as a lease less than 5 minutes after he said that.

Anthony was an amazing man, even though he definitely had some honesty issues, that I must make clear, I do not condone. I also believe that when you blur ethical lines, it will always come back to haunt you. This however isn't the purpose of this story. Anthony even had a form named after him called the "Rocco Must Sign Form." It was invented because Anthony would frequently tell customers to leave their lease turn-ins with him and not to worry about them. Anthony would then not tell the desk about remaining payments or anything that could mess up his deals having to do with "silly lease returns." We once had a Land Rover that the customers thought had been returned to Canada and it was sitting on our lot for 9 months and nobody noticed. This Land Rover incident happened years after the creation of the "Rocco Must Sign Form." A form I use to have to put in every deal I ever did for years when I would become a closer, never having told a customer a lie about their lease return. Anthony for some reason still didn't need to fill out his own form. Anthony really didn't like using his own form. The form was meant to make sure we knew what was happening with lease returns.

Anthony really was in jail when he invented the Product Specialist System we have all at least heard of by now.

It all started back in 2001, when Anthony was in jail for the 3rd time while working for the company. Back then all the salespeople closed their own deals. They all hated Anthony. Anthony would have 2 customers on test drives while closing a 3rd and greeting people he never met at the front with "great seeing you guys again, have a seat I'll be right with you." Everybody else was struggling. You'd think this would be great for Anthony. It wasn't. For a man that lived on the wrong side of the law, his glass house was made of some really thin glass for these guys. They were always trying to trip up Anthony instead of trying to sell cars themselves. As you can imagine, this frustrated the owner and Anthony. He kept getting arrested because the other salespeople kept calling his parole officer and probation officers and getting him re arrested over the years. The dealership's sales would decline drastically when Anthony was in jail.

So here he was in jail again, this couldn't keep happening. As

Anthony sat there thinking about what to do, he realized he was wasting his talent doing test drives and all the stuff he did other than closing deals. After all, Anthony didn't even know what size engines were in the different models and he didn't think that was important to know at all when it came to selling a car. Sometimes he would have to get Henry though, who was an awful closer at the time and sold 2-3 cars a month, to ask him about something a customer wanted to know about the product. Henry knew everything about the cars. Anthony would come and ask the same question twice in a row, it was literally impossible for Anthony to retain how many seats even came in a model. He was proud about it too.

What if I closed all the deals? Anthony thought to himself. He knew he had to tell the owner about his idea. What if Henry only did test drives and I closed his deals? Then maybe these guys wouldn't be so jealous of Anthony and they would like him around instead of constantly getting him arrested. He knew he had to sell it and he wasn't even sure if he would be allowed to return to work after being in jail again. Of course he would go to jail and keep his job 7 times. That's because Anthony kept things moving. He kept a competitive energy, he had an expensive habit, 3 kids and legal issues. If he could solve this problem, all the stars would finally line up. Anthony never made it to any sales meetings, always having the most amount of "old age money." Our GSM would tear up his old age checks in front of everybody at every sales meeting I ever attended when Anthony was working and not in jail, then drop them in the trash can by the door during the sales meeting. It was thousands of dollars. I heard Anthony once say "it's worth not sitting in those meetings," when he was just told he lost $2,500 one day. He only had to show up an hour earlier than he would to make the sales meetings.

Anthony had to do something. Pitching this idea when hoping to just still have his job was going to be a hard sell. How could Anthony get the owner to completely transform the way his Sales

Department ran? He had to come up with a plan; luckily he had some time in jail to think.

Anthony knew if it was his idea, it would never work. He had to make the owner think he came up with it. Little did he know, the Florida courts were about to do God's work for him. This was Anthony's 3rd driving on a suspended license charge along with a long list of other misdemeanors and felonies. #3 driving on a suspended license meant an automatic 5-year revocation in Florida for Anthony. So while he was coming up with a plot to invent the Product Specialist System and make the owner think it was his idea, the dealership's sales were already cut in half because Anthony was in jail. The owner was also about to be told Anthony can't drive a car on the lot again for 5 years.

So Anthony was coming up with some wild plot to start a fire in the dealership and the owner was just in need of his new idea. Anthony explained this to me just like that "I was going to start a fire." I asked him what that was going to do and his response was "I hadn't figured that part out yet." I'm serious. I actually used to pick Anthony up on the way to work from the work release facility and drop him off there after work for a period of time. I was asked to do this after being promoted to finance. When I first met Anthony, I would've thought he had a nice life and his act together. When I first met Anthony, he was sleeping at a work release facility.

Anthony was waiting for one of his daughters to sell a watch to make bail because it was the 24th of the month when he got arrested and we got wash out checks on the 10th. Anthony was usually full-on-broke, eating ramen noodles out of a Styrofoam cup by the 17th or 18th until the next wash day on the 10th. Anthony made about $25-30k/month back then too. The owner decided he needed to bail Anthony out to figure out a strategy because he couldn't lose half his sales to Anthony's unfortunate hard cocaine habit. The owner said he didn't really know if he was bailing Anthony out to take him out to the woods or to bring him back.

This is what is said to have happened:

Anthony: "Oh man, thanks for showing up, I was dying in there! I was only in there 4 days and I was running all the games, it was about to get deep. Anyway, there's going to be a fire in the dealership, boss."

Store Owner: "What...... what? Anthony, what do you mean there's going to be a fire?"

Anthony: "I just have a feeling; I have an instinct about this sort of thing."

Store Owner: "Anthony, I need to talk to you, you know they are revoking your driver's license right? You can't work as a salesman in a car dealership without a driver's license, Anthony."

Anthony: "That's hoopla! You can't run a dealership with the mucks you got, sir! I'm the only one that sells you cars! And there's going to be a fire anyway, they'll forget all about me."

Store Owner: "Who will forget about you, and what fire are you talking about Anthony?"

Anthony: "I got an idea. What if all the guys just test drove cars and then I... I just finished their deals for them?"

Store Owner: "So, you go to jail again and get out and I make you everybody's boss?"

Anthony: "Why not boss? Is this about being a perfect citizen or selling cars damnit?"

Store Owner: "Who else can close like you Anthony?"

Anthony: "You have one other talented guy and he sleeps in your showroom half the day."

Store Owner: "Ahmed?"

Anthony: "Yeah."

Store Owner: "I'm going to make you and Ahmed my closers and we will figure this out. You are right, I can't run the dealership with these sleepy mutts!Let's first talk about this fire, what are you talking about?"

Anthony: "What fire, I didn't say anything about a fire."

This all really happened.

When they got back to the dealership they went into the owners office and the conversation continues.

Anthony: "This is exactly what you need to do, this is why the fire isn't happening now."

Store Owner:"I thought you said what fire?"

Anthony: "Yeah what fire? Anyway boss, these guys you got, they're nothing but a bunch of Product Specialists! They don't know how to close! Except Ahmed and only when he isn't sleeping! You need a big change here, boss! You should have me up at the desk."

Store Owner: "Anthony I'm pretty sure you were going to start a fire in the dealership without me giving you the keys to the dealership, so that's never happening, you're nuts!"

Anthony: "Never?"

Store Owner: "Never!"

Anthony: "Ok, well how about I just close all the deals?"

Store Owner: "What did you just call them again... Product Specialists?"

Anthony: "Yeah they're nothing but a bunch of walking brochures!"

Store Owner: "Product Specialists, I kind of like that." "why not? That's what they already are!"

Anthony: "Wait you are going to call them that?"

Store Owner: "Why not? It sounds non-threatening."

Anthony: "That's what they all are, non-threatening to making anybody pay profit!"

Store Owner: "Ok Anthony, do you think you can go home and be back here at 9 am? I have to talk with Jay about how we are going to make this work."

Anthony: "Yes of course, can I borrow $500?"

Store Owner: "Go see Emily, she'll give you an advance."

This is how it all started. This is how Anthony Rocco successfully invented the Product Specialist System we've all heard of today. Of course Anthony and the owner had no idea that what they had just come up with would change and revolutionize our business as we know it, forever. Anthony was just trying to stay out of jail, sell cars, spend time with his family, and try to stop smoking crack. His solution to his temporary problem would be so wildly successful that it would soon gain national traction as the sales process of the new millennium. Anthony would continue to be arrested, but his idea would transform this dealership and dealerships across the nation, permanently and forever.

See what Anthony hadn't thought about, was how many problems his solution actually solved. Henry, and the other "Henrys", were great at test drives, being nice to the customers, and gaining trust, but they just weren't closers like Anthony and Ahmed. They were afraid to ask for money and had no idea how to gain the upper hand in a negotiation. They hated doing it too, though they would never admit that. Anthony and the owner would soon realize that they can train people to fulfill the Product Specialist role much quicker than they could train somebody in full A-Z car sales and the negotiation process. They could also recruit friendly, non-threatening people to do this job and mold them the way they wanted them, like they did with me. The most important training and the only semi-difficult objection a Product Specialist needs to overcome, is telling the customer that they do not and cannot talk numbers. After they overcome this objection, their job becomes fun and easy. The customer becomes relaxed and interested in the product. Their job is to find the car that the customer wants most and if they like, then they can talk to a Sales Manager about what it takes to buy or lease. The "if you like, you can talk to a Sales Manager afterwards..." is a diffusion tactic and a white lie, they will be talking to a manager after the Product Specialist lands them on "The Car." The customer is actually put at ease, believing this white lie and it allows them to "shop" without the financial pressure and common car buying fears occupying their headspace. This allows the customer to find their car and stay focused on the product first with their Product Specialist, who is mostly trained to extensively demo and fact find, then sit them down and put them on paper.

This dealership went from 8 total A-Z salespeople to 8 closers and 21 Product Specialists in 18 months. Was it just Anthony's system? Was it the economy? It couldn't be this simple. This dealership would go from selling 60 cars a month, Anthony selling 30 of them when he wasn't in jail, to selling 300 a month in about 18 months. It had to be something else. The market must've had a growth spurt. Something other than just creating this system, but it wasn't. It was Anthony's system. Everything ran smoother. The other closest new luxury car dealers, hadn't seen any type of comparable growth at all. In fact this was in the early 2000's and all of the other luxury and non-luxury new car dealers had remained stagnant at best. They had hit gold and thank God, because this is also why they would have a position for me in a couple years, a young kid that didn't know anything about sales.

Arguing diminished. He was able to do what he was best at doing. He was now helping Henry sell 10 cars instead of Henry selling 2-3 and wanting to kill him. Nobody wanted Anthony out of the dealership except maybe Ahmed and now the new closers, he closed everybody's deals. Ahmed would also quickly step up and close other people's deals. 18 months later when there were 8 Anthony's, and around 20 Product Specialists, thats when they hired me. They had already taken the best "Henry" and made him Training Director. His name was Fred. Fred was great at product knowledge, giving customers gifts and referring to himself as "Fred Clause" when he would go to service and get a bunch of mugs and hats to give away to customers while they were negotiating on the floor. Fred Clause is giving out hats to my customers and I'm introduced to this seamless process where they train me to meet and greet, drive the customers, then complete my write up, say "I have a deal," and go sit with my customers and shut the fuck up while Anthony does his thing. This was my first introduction to the car business. I wouldn't work at another dealership for 10 years. I would leave this dealership to move to California in 2014. Imagine my surprise when I was hiring kids with no train-

ing and dropping them onto a sales floor expecting them to negotiate their own deals. I had sat and watched a man that didn't
know how to tell the truth, usually harmlessly, and a magician
at closing deals, none the less, for months before I would go into
finance.

The only total green peas that wouldn't learn the art of
closing a car deal in this system were the few that just couldn't
shut the fuck up at the table. They never got past being able to
say, "this doesn't make sense to me but I'll roll with it." That's
how I learned fast. Anybody that grew up in this process has, at
a minimum, a massive amount of unused solely from watching
these guys do what they do with their customers, and shutting
the fuck up. Had I been competing with Ahmed and Anthony,
my mom would've been so right it's ridiculous. I would've been
eaten alive when I first started with these guys. Instead I was their
test drive guy. I was the "get the car ready" guy to these closers.
I was, however, also apprenticing. I gained this experience as an
apprentice because a part of the Product Specialist's job is to sit
with the customer and shut the fuck up while the closer closes. In
my situation, my closers, the dealership and I won huge with this
process. They got a great test drive bitch when I didn't know anything. This process would also soon create the highest producing
Finance Manager this dealership would ever have at the time, me.
They didn't have to pay me much back then either and rightfully
so, as just this opportunity alone for me would be responsible for
my entire career. I was 21 and had 2 months of experience when
I started in finance. I was setting dealership records for warranty
penetration and Lo-Jack sales 6 months into my career in the
business. I won the Lo-jack Caribbean vacation with 69 Lo-jack
sales my 12th month in the business.

Watching Anthony and Ahmed close my deals was the base
education I needed to go learn how to close finance products. I
had this base education from 2 months of test driving customers,
sitting there and shutting the fuck up in a volume dealership.

I would also be the one the customers would spill their anxieties to while Anthony or Ahmed were in the sales desk working the deal. The Product Specialist will almost always be trusted by the customer just on the basis that they are uninvolved with the financial part of the transaction. The customers in turn usually view their Product Specialist as their little puppy that shows them around and that they can confide in, and they do. Your Product Specialists will also get this look into the customers psychology that the Ahmeds and Anthonys already understand. In the heat of the battle, first as a spectator, before going in to battle themselves. I had little realizations that would've taken me years to understand thinking back to what I saw these closers do. I wouldn't have made it in this dealership at 21-years-old before this system. Instead I was hired with this system and I would end up being the highest producing Finance Manager for 2 years straight in this dealership, starting in only a matter of months from my 2 month experience as a Product Specialist. Maybe I paid a ton of attention and was a sharp kid to begin with, etc. Maybe. Let's just say that's true. To truly look at the system lets look outside me.

When hiring an A-Z salesperson you are looking for multiple skillsets. You most likely want people with experience, which we also know comes with bad habits.

"You look like you're the hire but I won't ever really know until I actually hire you. I'll know your first few days though if I do..."

-True words from a GM hiring me

When hiring a Product Specialist, you are looking for that person that "wowed" you most recently at the cell phone store or even the Chik-Fil-A drive thru. It could've been a bartender or a theatre usher. Age doesn't matter. It could be a long-time teacher that wants to make money. Every once in a while, we all go "wow that guy could kill it for me" when we are out and about in the world. Once you have a structure and processes to drop this person in, you will feel confident to make that recruiting attempt every time you come across potential talent. You will also have the available space at all times. You will also never be done hiring. I almost didn't write that you will never be done hiring because I know some out there imagine a full staff that is with them for a long time and one day want to stop hiring. This is almost possible, but we will still always be growing and hiring. People move and move on and lives change. You are always hiring if your dealership is growing. I had to leave this dealership to further my career. Jay and Barry are still sitting in the same chairs as they were behind the desk in 2004 when I was in my first month of finance.

All a green pea Product Specialist needs when hired into this process, as far as skillset, is the ability to meet and greet combined with common sense customer service. You shouldn't be looking for the worlds' greatest closers at all. You should be looking for inexperienced, positive and enthusiastic people that want to make money. Because you aren't hiring for closing ability, dotting I's and crossing T's will come easier to your new hires than it is for your Anthony Roccos who are notoriously bad at filling out forms that are even named after them. This is the person you give the responsibilities of checking vin numbers, making sure the car is clean, asking for the survey, grabbing the tag from finance, giving your customer a proper delivery, following up and all the general process stuff after Anthony swoops in and closes the deal.

Once you implement this system, it actually isn't easy to tell if your 20 car guys will make good closers. I think it all has to do with personality type and of course a desire which relates to how much they pay attention and want to learn those skills. A lot of guys are very comfortable being Product Specialist's forever and have no interest in being closers. It's a great job. Sometimes I think, "man it wouldn't be all that bad to just test drive and make 120k," like many of them do, year in and year out. The record at this store is 47 cars now for one Product Specialist in a month. The first bonus is at 12 car sales. It was at 7 when I started. They still make that money. One of them made 120k+ for over a decade and speaks very poor English. This store still has 8 Product Specialist's that worked next to me as a Product Specialist in 2004. They are still always hiring. The turnover is extremely low.

The main success for this process ultimately boils down to the division of labor it provides. Instead of training people A-Z, we are able to train people to just be great at doing test drives, getting people to paper, being your customers' best friend and finding "The Car" ("The Boat" or "The Bike") they would buy today if everything else was perfect. Once they prove themselves at this level, they are awarded an opportunity to close if they want to, when a position opens up. Then we invest in pencil training with them. Then we invest in their negotiation skills. This also provides more organization to your dealership and more time available to management when you are only training your clear proven choices to move up to the second half of selling a car. They will only have the habits they created in your dealership. They are also prepared to carry on the system as they grew up in it themselves. This store has 14 closers today. 13 of them were once Product Specialists. They all have 30% closing ratios. Ahmed has a 45% closing ratio.

Having Anthony close all the deals, and having all the "Henrys" do all the test drives, was like hitting oil. Everything improved, even CSI. Ahmed and Anthony could actually get a little more wild with the customers. The customers had their little puppy dog Product Specialist they trusted and didn't want to let down now. A 3rd baseman in their court. The Product Specialist is who you train to tell the customer at the end of the deal "It is my survey only, it only affects me, please give me all 10's." It was like butter overnight. Jay, the GSM, was the one who would come to refine the system and turn it into what it really is today. He would come up with "I have a deal" (next chapter) which became the oil in this new machine. Jay was all of a sudden training 70% of the team to "never talk numbers" and the other 30% advanced closing techniques (confusing, manipulating, and berating the shit out of the closers in order for them to make money). The closers now only have two duties, "Get a commitment" & "Bump them". Now from behind the desk, Jay and Barry sell 500+ cars a month and they work with 12 or 13 total salespeople (only closers); the entire rest of the store is only seen in the sales office saying "I have a deal!" Incredible! Some of the closers in this dealership will close up to 80+ deals per month. All they do is close and move on, follow up responsibilities are placed almost 100% solely on the Product Specialist. Your Pay-Plans should allow for your closers to be a lot less tied to CSI results than your Product Specialists. This allows your closers to close while forcing your Product Specialists to keep your customers happy.

I'd be hired in when this process was already built up to what it remains today in this dealership. 16 years have passed, and I could go do that job the same way I was trained in 2004. The old paper up log managed by the receptionist is now managed by a software and that's about the extent of the changes in this dealership's sales process. This dealership thrives from this one process. I would go on to see and even create processes this dealership could use. This goes to show you that you could have everything right and we know there is room to improve, but we aren't struggling so we don't realize the opportunities we have to continue to grow at massive rates with other simple processes that solve so much.

This process was refined from Anthony Rocco's original idea to become the mysterious to some, the "we tried that, it didn't work" to others, and "there is no other way" to the ones that have already implemented this process. If you aren't doing this process and let's say you have "Delivery Specialists" but your salespeople are closing their own deals from the day they start or even closing their own deals now in their 2nd month, look out at that person on your showroom-floor and ask yourself how they and your dealership would benefit with this process in place. Who's your best closer? Imagine this person closing all of your deals and your new salesperson only test-driving and doing the rest of the sales process in your dealership. Mainly, the customer service portion of the sale. I could write the "customer service potion" if I wanted.

The division of labor in the Product Specialist System is the same theory behind what The McDonalds brothers came up with and Ray Kroc saw so much potential in. It's what CarMax and Texas Direct do on their recon lines. It only makes sense that you have one person doing test drives and "sitting people" all day and another person going back and forth to your sales desk "shutting people" all day. Think about it. It's truly golden when implemented and not "tried". It's a division of labor. Dividing labor responsibilities is the theory behind a manufacturing line. When labor is divided within any process, efficiency is always instantly boosted. The Product Specialist System is really just that concept applied to the steps to the sale.

All I ask is that you DO NOT "try" this process. If you are going to "try it", re-read this chapter again. You need to "implement it", which means there is no going back. Our industry is better off as a whole. Our customers are happier, and happier to pay a little more because they get that friendly Product Specialist that always picks up their phone. This Product Specialist is much more likely to be at your dealership in a few years or 20, than if you hired them for A-Z car sales. Their job is to actually care about your customer, they should have zero pressure on them to "make gross" outside of not circumventing the system and talking numbers. This is the biggest no-no. It's the most important expectation you lay on them so that they can take care of your customers. Customer service only.

Don't try it, implement it, please.

"I HAVE A DEAL"

"You can't get these ingrates to say 4 simple fucking words... "I Have A Deal..."

-Jay, 2004

I've already told you about this if you read the introduction about my run-in with this process on my first deal. Now we are going to meet the inventor of the "I have a deal" process. His name is Jay. Jay was GSM when Anthony and the owner came up with the Product Specialist System behind Jay's back. Not that Jay cared, he was actually excited to hear about it and give it a go and not be blamed for how it turned out. He was loving it when it first started, he didn't have to deal with the Henrys and the other "weak sucks" anymore. He had Anthony and Ahmed, The Great Singh, who he could beat up on all day, on all the customers, it was great.

One thing started happening that just pissed Jay off though as soon as Anthony's system was implemented. It was working great but Jay was pissed about one thing specifically that was an obvious result of the new system. The new Product Specialists, now not having to close deals would come into the sales office and hand Ahmed or Anthony their guest card and say, "good luck, they aren't buying shit" or "they have a so and so trade they think is worth 100k, haha". Jay found himself everyday over and over again lecturing these guys, throwing them out of the office and telling them to shut up. They'd mostly respond to him with, "he's the closer, I don't know" or "isn't he supposed to close it anyway" and just plain salty remarks from these newly laterally moved test drivers making $350-$500 a car.

56

"These guys are fucking whiners, you'd think they'd be pumped making $500 a fucking car and I got Ahmed closing all their deals. Instead they're whining like a bunch of bitches and fucking up their own deals by coming in here and kicking these guys in the nuts before they go out on their T.O. What the fuck?"

So, Jay thought about it for a while and pondered a no speaking rule. Threw it around and came up with his aha moment. "I got it... I have a deal!"

He calls the meeting midday. "All Product Specialists to the sales desk." Everybody floods into the sales office. "Alright listen up, from now on because it seems some of you whine way too much for my nerves and one day one of you is gonna piss me off and make me do something I regret. We have a new rule to put into place; from now on, none of you, unless you're a tie (a closer because they wore ties, Product Specialists wore and still wear short sleeved collared shirts), are allowed to speak in this office. You're only allowed to say 4 words in this office, which are "I have a deal." I don't care if your customer just showed you their bank account with a negative balance and their credit score as of today has a 3 handle, when you come into this fucking office, you say, "I have a deal." You put your guest card right here on the desk and you get the fuck out and go sit with your customer. Is that clear?" There was an eruption of "Yes Jay." "Any questions? Good. That's it."

And that was it. If you go to this dealership today and stay anywhere around or inside this sales desk area, you will see the Product Specialists come in one door, say "I have a deal" and go out the other door. You could stand there for months and you won't see a Product Specialist with a guest card in their hand, in and around that office say anything other than "I have a deal" and get the fuck out of the office and go sit with their customers. Unless of course you catch another me on his 1st day and that would literally be it.

I would work in one dealership after this one with a variation of the Product Specialist System and it was the last dealership I actually worked in. We did not have the "I have a deal" process when I started. We consistently had the "my customer isn't buying today, but go talk to them" problem, also when I started. Once we implemented "I have a deal," you never heard it again. Sometimes you can see it in a Product Specialist's face when they are having a bad day or deal, they really want to say something, but don't. I've been there. When you get home, you are glad you didn't speak whatever weakness medicine was flowing through your veins at that moment. This process actually makes your people smarter! Oh the power in shutting the fuck up.

It was truly amazing. "Clockwork" is the best way to explain what Jay had created. One of my favorite Jay lines of all time was "this isn't a democracy here, this is a dictatorship." Jay is kindhearted, has a spine and stands up for his people behind their backs and trashes them to their faces non-stop if they can handle it, which of course I could. Only Jay could say the stuff he said to me. I would never operate a dealership without Jay's "I have a deal" process. It's so simple and solves so many problems.

Once again, please DO NOT "try it" and implement it, please.

Section 2: Step 5 Processes

STEP 5 PROCESSES INTRO:

Step 5 Processes Intro: More Spreadsheets?, Double Data Entry?, Systems That Don't Talk To Each Other? No — Accurate Data, Teamwork, Laser Focus On What Matters and Pure Seamlessness In Processes.

This is when I get to tell you all about how I invented the greatest digital desk-log that will ever exist, seriously. First we have to start with Mahmoud, he was the original inventor of the Finance Department. More recently in his now very elder state he was the inventor of not selling anything and lowering your customers' payment without you knowing until they got home and blaming it on you. Yeah, that guy. As you can imagine, one day Mahmoud was being fired but first he was taking everybody with him. We'd all find out loudly over the pager in a locked finance office with only Mahmoud in it for about 2 minutes before we figured how to turn off the paging system with customers listening. Mahmoud would roll everybody under the bus for anything he knew about anybody, especially our GSM who had just fired him. Mahmoud would eventually come out after saying "I'm not going anywhere" from inside his locked office for a couple hours. I asked our GSM at the time "are you just going to leave him in there?" He said, "he'll come out eventually, at least we got the pager turned off." Mahmoud would come out... eventually to re-enact the scene from Jerry Maguire where he would scream "I'm leaving" as if it was his decision and actually ask if anybody wanted to come with him. Of course unlike Jerry

Maguire, nobody went with him. Mahmoud had been around for a long time and nobody actually knew how long. Mahmoud was the only person I ever met working at a dealership where nobody knew how long he had been working there. He was the verified inventor of the Finance Department and must've been around 105 years old or older. I'd actually run into Mahmoud about a year later, when he was my uber driver and never saw him again after that.

It all started of course before Mahmoud was fired. Before I get into this, I have to tell you that I have a very high patience for finance being slow etc. I never expected Finance Managers to walk in my footsteps and be fast. That did very well for my popularity amongst the sales team, but finance is not about going fast. I do not, however believe in a Finance Manager ever asking for things missing in deals before they go meet the customer. The customer's time is moving at 2 hours a second after they say yes and they are waiting for this big bad Finance Manager they have no idea is actually scared of them too. It's ridiculous and we will go over it in the 3rd chapter of this section.

So Mahmoud was not a "calculating, predictable, go slow because I know there's a cash deal or go slow because I'm selling stuff" type of Finance Manager. Mahmoud was completely unpredictable. I have a hunch he was just fucking with people. All of a sudden when he was missing $5 of change from me making the food run; my customers that were just put in his office were gone, but he got a contract signed and sold the car for 2k less than we agreed on. Or he would take 5 hours and not sell anything or take 6 and get a full menu on nail salon owners. It never made any sense. He would throw a tantrum and start complaining about totally unrelated things like a 4-year-old, and our GM would always tell us we need to "know how to work with Mahmoud." It was a total mess.

I wanted to actually somehow track this and show how

many deals Mahmoud was losing the dealership. Little did I know, I would venture down 1,000 rabbit holes from this first experiment of mine. I had just learned how to use the fancy CRM (you know which one). I hated all the CRM's and all the computer systems except for the DMS, because I wouldn't want to draw a lease by hand. Everything else, I loved using paper. I'm a millennial they say, but I didn't have cell phones in my high school, and I think that's where they should've drawn that line. I relate much more to being completely frustrated by machines and screens than I do to a behind the back texting 8-year-old. When I first used a DMS for years, I didn't explore anything past knowing where to go for the things I needed to do, print forms etc. That had changed by now. My GM had put me in control of the Internet Department and I had realized that these guys were all able to completely fool me about their activity and what they were doing. I would have no idea what deals they were even working unless I learned what they were doing in the computer. Their customers would just show up and ask for them. When I was first in charge of this department, I was totally an overpaid hall monitor. That wasn't going to be ok with me, even if it was ok with my GM. They were on the phones, but everything they had came from the internet. I hated computers, but I had to figure it all out. My GM did this to me on purpose and told me that when he did it. "You need to learn the Internet Department Philip, this is the future of our business." I learned the CRM because I had to in this situation and that would be one of the greatest things I ever did.

My original idea had nothing to do with a desk-log, and if you had asked me if we used the desk-log in the fanciest CRM (you know the one), I would've laughed at you. I was now the leading expert in the Dealership with the fanciest CRM, tasked to call them with all questions and issues. Nobody in our store used the desk-log inside this fancy CRM (now you really know the one).

All I wanted to do was log time in and time out of finance and which Finance Managers got the deals. That's all I wanted to do. I pulled out a piece of paper and started drawing. Of course my guys now are a bunch of computer geeks and are like "let's do it on the computer." My mind had literally just been opened to the idea of now using these things for something. I literally protested the CRM's, e-contracting and all of the tech changes during the first half of my career. I was that guy. I was ok with the idea now and I trusted these guys, I was becoming a bit of a geek myself complaining all the way there. I was once again just trying to show how many deals Mahmoud was actually losing and how much time it was taking for him to lose these deals. Customers would never complain about Mahmoud. I think it was because he was 105, so it was as if Mahmoud wasn't really Mahmoud to the GM. Mahmoud was probably costing our 700-car store, with 5 finance guys at the time, 50-75 deals/month easily. It was that crazy. He'd take 100 deals and end up with 25 at the end of the month in his name. The other Finance Managers all around 70-120. We all just dealt with it, it was totally crazy. Giving your deal to Mahmoud was like Russian roulette. You might end up fired, "this could be your last day, Mahmoud has your deal" was actually a common catch phrase we would retell each other. Multiple people had actually lost their jobs in connection to a deal they did with Mahmoud. Mahmoud would never get blamed or even talked to, it was as if the problem didn't exist. It's difficult to even paint Mahmoud, he was so unique to anything I've ever seen. Remember my first closer was Anthony Rocco. Our GM at the time didn't believe anything anybody told him about Mahmoud, after all Mahmoud was the original inventor of the Finance Department. I think our GM liked bragging about that and left out the fact that he was now a 400 per copy guy.

So Anaj pulls up "Google Docs", I really didn't even know how to use Google Docs at the time. This was 2014. He just numbers lines and at the top puts "time in", "time out" and hooks that up to a timer so when we stop it, it calculates the time out. I said "ok that's pretty cool." I jump in and turn it into more of an old school desk-log across the top, not purposefully at all. I just put stuff I thought I'd ask about the deals. I said, "fancy CRM name doesn't have this and you actually got me thinking, lets log all the customers that you guys get in here." I did this because I was 7 or 8 months deep into learning the fancy CRM and I wanted specific data easily accessible.

It was incredible what happened. Now I could see with ease how many people my team actually got into the store that day, how many went to finance, how long finance took, who the Finance Manager was etc, etc. Now I'm joking when I say I invented the first digital desk-log that works, because of course I now know that many dealers and dealer groups have made something similar. I've now seen many other dealers that have created something similar outside of their CRM along the same lines of my original desk-log. Every one of these systems does things the CRM's do not. This I would come to learn is because of the extreme disconnect between software developers and the people that actually work inside a dealership.

What I did next is, I got obsessed. I got obsessed with how this single spreadsheet Anaj had built in 30 minutes, was helping me stay more organized and giving me more information much quicker than the CRM that was supposed to sell cars for me, at least according to the fancy CRM Rep with my GM nodding yes in his office. I got obsessed with what else we could do from scratch to solve problems we were having, using this very simple desk-log.

We became super-efficient with this desk-log I had started obsessing over. I put a little column for "T.O" if I talked to them when they were here, so when going back, I'd know if I met them or not when calling them. My department was selling 120-160 cars by ourselves with 5 or 6 people, depending on the month. My guys were A-Z, I did not have Product Specialists. I got more obsessed. I wanted to see from across the room how many sales we had out, so late one night I decided to make the sold lines red, it worked. When my guys' deals would leave finance, and I was working 2 or 3 other deals on a busy Saturday, I would see my guys turn their lines red, and I'd know "we have another one out of the box" from across the room, while I was still with customers. Very shortly after, I decided that when we send deals to finance, we should turn the lines yellow, that way from across the room, I know how many are in finance. The way my team and I were communicating with each other with this thing, I had now put weeks of time into using, made the rest of the store, which sold 600 between retail and fleet, look chaotic.

We had originally been going for data on Mahmoud, and of course we had lost track of that. Not only that, I swear the day we started using this thing, Mahmoud became a new man, at least for a little while. We all of a sudden had zero Mahmoud issues, though he was still frightening to hand your customers to one by one. Mahmoud was doing deals and there weren't issues. It was like the eye of a hurricane and we all kind of knew it, it was so weird. I imagine somebody told Mahmoud what we were doing, so that makes sense, but it's still incredible to me that the same person possessed the ability to be coherent, seriously. It became a nonissue pretty quikly in our fast-paced dealership; we didn't even think about it again until Mahmoud came back and relinquished whoever was possessing his body for probably 6-7 weeks. Before the Legend of Mahmoud returned we were up in sales, a lot and quickly. Now just to be clear I was never trying to say this desklog fixed Mahmoud. I will always say it was responsible for us immediately selling 20%+ more units, and I'll go to my grave on that. It became a digital dry erase leaderboard for write-ups and starting at the write-up for my team. You had 2 chances to blank now. Not selling a car is one thing. Not even getting somebody to paper is another. This thing was now in front of our faces all day. If Sam got 4 people to paper today, and one of my guys did nothing for the last 2 days, he started hustling, you get it. Organically they were now counting write-ups aka: "Step-5's." I had accidentally created a Frankenstein trying to put Mahmoud's terrorism to an end. It wouldn't be long until retail wanted to do whatever I was doing, and of coarse our GM would find out and that wouldn't be fun for me at all.

It's a Friday, I'll never forget this Friday, and I'm supposed to come in at 8 am, so I wake up around 5:30. I see a voicemail from my GM, I think that's rare. He usually just texts "do you have a sec," which means come to my fucking office now. I listen to it and he says "Phil, before you come into the dealership today, come to my office as soon as you can." What the hell did I do? It was my day off before, so for all I knew, it could've been anything. I go into his office and he's on the phone, so I sit down. When he gets off the phone he says "hold on" and he calls in the controller and pretty much every high-level person he could find and then all the Sales Managers and Finance Managers. He proceeds to put my creation I had put months into up on his screen and asks, "can anybody tell me what this is?" I immediately go "that's my desk-log." A dozen people were there that didn't need to be as I got spit yelled at in front of all of them. He was so uninvolved with the minutia of the day to day, he didn't even know about Mahmoud. Honestly I never in a million years thought logging our deals on a spread-sheet would be such an insult to our GM. He would ask me a few more questions before proceeding to tell me what I did violated all types of laws, was stupid etc. I was basically sitting there in my head going "I'm going to spit back at you if you keep spitting in my face in a second because I'm pretty sure I'm getting fired." As I'm seriously heating up to make a really bad decision, because this was overkill and I was definitely overtly ganged up on here, like magic a good person comes to my rescue. Ricky speaks up and says, "Boss the only people that can see that are his internet people, we have been wanting to use it recently because it seems to be helping them a lot, we think this is why they are doing so well." Our GM respected Ricky, but there was also an air in the room now of "you're a mental patient if you keep abusing Phil." Maybe not from the controller, she brought her shotgun loaded and double checked it a couple times while I was sitting there, but the management team stuck up for me with energy for a minute.

He tried to ask a couple people in the room, including Ricky, to explain it to him, he was still fuming at me and at this point, we all know it's just because he didn't know about it. They all tell him to ask me, because they don't really know. I start explaining it to him and we immediately get into an argument that everything I'm telling him my desk-log does, we are supposed to be doing out of the fanciest CRM, you know the one. I didn't know what I know now, so I actually said, "well I don't really know where to do this out of the fanciest CRM". He of course responds in front of everybody in the room who all immediately start laughing out loud "aren't you the Internet Director?" Long story short, I was beaten into oblivion, told not to use the desk-log and to do whatever it was we were doing in the fanciest CRM. I was to report back to him how it's going, the last part being the most promising part. He let everybody go and then lectured me about leadership for a while.

I was pretty devastated as you can imagine. I just wanted to explain to him why this was working so well and why we should even use it in retail too. I was frightened he would fire me on the spot if I brought it up again and if he didn't, I would be subjected to more spit yelling and abuse. So I decided to sit for hours on hold with the fanciest CRM's Customer Service Department having them walk me through how to do what I was trying to do. Most of the times I'd get questions like "why are you trying to do that?" Or statements like "our system doesn't do that" or "it isn't meant to do that." I learned a lot going through this about a disconnect that started to become very clear to me. I was in my reality, sitting there trying to sell cars and I was on the phone with people that had no clue what that is like. I'll never forget sitting on hold, while I'm sending out pencils on $50,000 cars trying to get the fanciest CRM to do something I had just fixed with a spreadsheet. I don't give up, so I started trying to use the fanciest CRM for what our system was doing and telling all the

DEALERSHIP PROCESS SECRETS

guys they had to do these 55 different things 100% of the time and we would get it all back out of the fanciest CRM. You already know that never happened. It was just one of the most frustrating weeks of my life, which of course, as usual, was probably one of the most educational weeks as well. It was also the beginning to the education I was about to give myself by asking questions and of course... more tinkering.

You already know what I did next, I used it anyway. I woke up one day after all of this and already having had a few conversations with our GM, where "No" was still "No." I realized "I live in Los Angeles, I'm good at what I do, I can get 3 jobs today if I want, I have to keep using this thing." I knew I was right. I felt like the scene in the movie the Social Network when they said, "we don't know what it is yet." I didn't know what it was yet and I decided to break the rules.

I called a meeting and told my guys to use it on their phone only and that we are using it. I barely got any friction and I told them all I would take the fall and they can all say I made them do it. We did it, even cooler, the 6 of us did it for months without anybody else knowing and the incident became a thing of the past.

We would joke with retail that we were using it, but they would never had believed I had the balls. We were kicking ass and nobody but us knew why. It became our scoreboard; we could leave and know what was going on, because we made it so easy to update. I would learn so many things.

Eventually, one of my guys would tell one of the other Sales Managers, he thought in confidence, who would immediately tell our GSM, who would pull me into an office and say "I'm just talking to you before I tell him and you're fired." At this point I just spilled the beans about how I felt. I told him I didn't care if they fired me, they were dead wrong, etc. I even asked my GSM if I could just go and spare the spit yelling. It was over. I was definitely done. Ricky couldn't save me this time.

Our GM comes in and I'm the one that's irritable and disgruntled now, I say "come on I don't even want to hear it, give me my sales license, let's call it a wrap." He says, "sit down." He says, "show me what you made." I say, "ok,"pretty hesitant to pull it up. I was over the entire situation and ready to go. I was always ok with the fact that everyday could be my last, it's true no matter who you are or where you are. I didn't care and I was emotional. I showed him and told him how I felt for the first time, laying it all out. Had anybody else heard what I said to him, about him, I wouldn't have worked there. He had let our GSM out. We talked for hours about every aspect of everything. From the unimportant, like how what I had done made him feel, to the important, like what I think this thing can actually do for the dealership. He's skeptical and still mad. I think he also realized that I was most likely going to quit if he didn't fire me, maybe not that day, but soon if he didn't give it a shot. I was obsessed with what I had done with my system, I could find another paycheck.

We sat there as he negotiated with himself before he said, "Ok I want to try it then." I'll be honest, my eyes almost teared in front of him. He was now, for the first time, a human being when he could my emotions, and he said, "I think this is going to be good, do you think you can set it up now?" I said "yes" and all of a sudden probation was over. It was so exciting; the other 4 Sales Managers were excited too, because they knew I had to be on to something. They couldn't believe I still used it after the first incident.

What happened next would end up being a total disaster. Our GM said "take tomorrow off, go rest, come back and help us all use this thing of yours."

I knew what I had created didn't need instructions to use.

Everybody knew we were just logging all of our people and the system was programmed to do the rest. I thought that what we were doing would just transfer over to retail easily. I would spend my day off answering the questions about what I thought was the simple self-explanatory stuff and it was fun. I was at home in my sweats talking to the guys, telling them how to use my system I had built. I got lost in time and eventually worked the whole day from home essentially and was pumped up about it. I was so excited to go to work the next day; little did I know what I would be walking into. I didn't understand it at first and wouldn't figure it out for about 10-days, but retail had at least 10x what we had been putting on the log and they weren't selling 10x the amount of cars. It seems so simple now, it wasn't, and it isn't in most dealerships.

Retail was simply putting every up on the log, it just became this big huge disorganized looking sheet with some sales and some in finance. It wasn't the same. My guys had a sort of competition because the bar for them to get people in was relatively higher than a walk-in customer, I started to think. It was not easy to figure out. I finally, without pondering the steps to the sale, came in at it backwards and asked, "what if retail stopped putting everybody on there and only put the customers they've gotten to test drive?" This was a great start. They were of course treating my system like the CRM and putting everybody who would give them a name and number on our log. It was cluttered, and I would eventually learn there was a lot more wrong than that. It was a huge improvement just putting the people that test drove and beyond on their log. It started to work for them. The guys were getting more test drives organically overnight. We had created a second bar in Retail the way I had in internet. It used to be "how many did you sell today, yesterday?" Now it was "how many people did so and so get in today?", and "how many did everybody sell today?", in internet. In retail it was "how many test drives did you get today" because it was all right there, easy to read, made by me, with the stuff we actually wanted to look at. It was addictive. "How many red did you get today?" I heard one Sales Manager ask, referring to the red we change the line to when they come out of finance. I had built something that changed the dealership, I wasn't ever intending to do that, it felt incredible.

The desk-log was still cluttered in retail and I couldn't figure it out. I spent nights awake thinking about the difference between internet and retail and thinking it didn't make sense that they were that much different. I had started to calculate closing ratios with the information we had and retail was much lower than internet. Luckily I knew it wasn't due solely to my superior closing abilities, so I kept thinking. I remembered "steps to the sale" and couldn't even remember what dealership I was in when I saw it. I immediately Googled it and if you Google it, it comes right up. Not for auto sales, but there are steps to the sale. It jumped right out at me "addressing objections." It was the negotiation. Everybody we were putting on our log was negotiating. Retail had a considerably large amount of customers test driving and leaving without entering this stage. It was the sit down. It was the same, we had just missed it.

Of course the other managers thought I was nuts and didn't want to change what was working so I had to change the entire log to make them abide. I added a step column and just told them anything below a step 5 isn't allowed on the log and that goes for internet too." We would only have a few customers in the Internet Department that would come in without numbers already, so we were already doing it that way. It only made sense. This was when things really kicked off.

The competition now started with "getting people to a table" in retail and then how many you sold. Your name only ended up on the log if you sat people down to negotiate. You could test drive all day. That was the step where our log started. As soon as retail did this, they actually had more legitimate write-ups and less clutter. The next thing that happened was like watching dinosaurs drive cars. The Finance Managers started keeping it up on their screens. I had been in finance pretty recently, but I didn't get why they even wanted it at first. I felt like I created a sort of illicit commodity inside one dealership. I didn't realize how useful it was for finance yet either. They now were able to see the showroom from their offices. They were all of a sudden able to see the deals working because this thing stayed updated by the second. I didn't even know about update speed yet and without it this would've never happened in finance. Google Docs updates in seconds, this was crucial and is still crucial to the Daily Desk. None of the fancy CRM's understand this, hence the fastest update speed available is 3 minutes. We have a graphic at centraldesking.com that illustrates this serious problem. The Daily Desk updates every 3 seconds, which means if you change something, it changes on every screen within 3 seconds and without refreshing. This I know now and understand well, I didn't then at all, it was totally taken for granted and unnoticed. The Finance Managers would now always know whose deal was who's, because they'd be sitting in the back together looking at all of them and watch the next one turn yellow. Cut and dry whose deal it is whether they were hoping it was or wasn't. Did I really just solve finance rotation? I'm thinking I really did.

They also became more prepared all around because they always knew what was coming. The director decided he would put their initials in as the Finance Manager in the Finance Manager column, because he can use it to run rotation as they drop. He would easily speak to the bank and know when deals were coming by watching them get marked approved on the desk-log I had built. It was seamless, something that previously seemed impossible, was now seamless. I had made sales crack. It was awesome. What I would invent next would change the dealership sales follow-up game forever.

THE FOLLOW-UP POTION

"I just called so and so from Saturday, he bought from somewhere else, I did all my tasks in my CRM."

-A Salesman, Somewhere, every 30 seconds

Meet Alex, the man that sparked the idea that would create the Hot Sheet. Alex wasn't on my team or in my department and I would have never brought him or hired him, at this moment in time at least. I would've fired him if he was on my team. I may have also hired him back easily had he begged a little, remember Jay, my first GSM. At first he was just another random hire that looked goofy and young. These were my favorite hires just because I could relate to starting in the business so young and I felt I knew how to mold them. My favorite thing to tell candidates brand new to our business was "you can and will make a lot of money if you eat and sleep this business and become obsessed with it." Then I tell them, however, in a decade from now, whether you made 4 grand or 8 grand in a month, which will terrorize you in the moment, won't matter at all. What will matter is what you take from your experiences in this business. You will learn so much about people and you will be able to use what you learn, in this business or in any other career or business. Also, the work ethic you develop now, you will take with you anywhere you go, so make decisions like people are watching. Obviously this advice is catered more to the younger hire but applicable to any age if new to our business because our business is so special.

Later I would come to find out things about Alex that would impress me. I didn't hire him, so I didn't know much and he wasn't on my team. Once again if you're in a volume dealership, you can work on the sales desk and unfortunately almost never even speak to a new hire that only lasts a couple weeks. I noticed Alex right at his first couple weeks. It seemed the sales staff had a made a joke of him and he was engaging the attention. I did the morning meetings at this dealership 2 or 3 times a week and the first thing I noticed was Alex would show up late, then right after the meeting go shave in the bathroom. I was always of the mentality to focus on the guys that wanted to work. My biggest pet peeve with my GSM's or GM's or even owners when I was a GM, was the focus on what the people that didn't want to work were doing. I have a guy standing in front of me trying to sell a car and I'm being told to go write somebody up that took a 2 hour lunch or won't leave the smoking area. I don't care about that guy, I hope he puts in his 2 weeks and I'll let him go on the spot. I am focused on the people that want to be here. Our time is way too limited. An extra car deal is usually the same as an extra 20 minutes of free time for a good desk guy. That was so frustrating to me and I feel the same frustration when I see parents focusing on the bad kid instead of the good kid. I don't think laziness and lack of care should be paid any attention or given any energy. I'm aware it's there and when it crosses my path and I have the opportunity, I clip it immediately and effectively. I'd rather wait in the bushes for it to cross my path and take action than go hunting for it. It's a distraction because my attention pays way more ROI focusing on the people that are trying to sell and feed their families. This strategy I believe to be extremely effective and you will actually create a culture of non-lazy people. You will be respected by the people you help and then seen as somebody that will take out the trash before it even smells, without ever making a big deal about it beforehand. I'm not saying don't give poor performers second or even fifth chances. I'm saying the attention we pay to the negative can be cut down by 90% on average. I'm also saying that when the behavior doesn't get attention paid to it, it dies. It suddenly becomes not cool at all. Remember, a lot of people consider just getting others distracted a win. "Alex is smoking where he shouldn't be" was said to me. I returned with what I know about what the person telling me this is supposed to be doing "did you get in touch with Mr. and Mrs. smith yet?" I pay no attention to this person, and will not allow this nonsense to occupy my headspace. Don't feed a negative behavior. It may even occupy my headspace, but I don't share that to anybody and I solve it without anybody seeing any attention paid to it.

Alex was different. As soon as I started hearing the stories and seeing how he behaved with my own eyes and the things he said, I quickly started to think we had another Mahmoud.

The first thing I heard that allowed me to break my rules and give into the negative attention was when one of my guys came to me laughing telling me about how Alex had delivered a customer's car this morning, and on the way he "picked up a friend" in the customers brand new delivery. When he dropped the brand new car off, the customer said there was ash in it and a burn hole from a cigarette on the passenger side of the car. Just to be clear, people actually got fired from this store for very little. This wasn't one of the "you can't get fired here" dealerships. I'm not even sure anybody even talked to Alex about this because he was causing so much other drama, it went unnoticed. In the same week I found out that 2 separate female customers had gone on our yelp and said variations of "Alex sexually harassed me while I was buying my car." It was absurd. He was also still late everyday. He wasn't mine and his manager didn't seem to care, he kept saying "that's Alex."

I was at the desk closing alone one night when Alex brought me a deal. Alex had no business working any numbers with customers. I was the Internet Director at the time, so I did some really nasty looking deals. It's late, I was working several deals and Alex's customers seemed very difficult. I get to the bottom quick on this one and tell Alex "here's the deal, this is as good as it will get, try to get more if you can." He finally tells me he has 2k down and $450/mo. I prepare the deal and give it over to finance. I end up called into the office and the customer was saying Alex told them $500 down and $350 a month. Alex comes in and lies right in front of the customer. 11 or 12 years in the business at this point and this was a first for me. Alex had negotiated a fake deal, told me he had something else, put his customers in finance, then lied right to the customers' face and I knew it because the customer immediately was throwing his hands around saying "this is a fucking joke." Alex would later admit he did that too with a Steve Urkel type of "did I do that?" vibe.

Alex would actually still be at this dealership slightly after I left. I ended up really liking Alex. I found out he had a sick mom, no dad and was actually supporting his family living in a one bedroom, acting like this too, but he was 19 years old.

The next morning, I would explain what happened to Alex's manager Dan who would repeat what he said before, "That's Alex." I was confused. Unless he told Alex to do that to me, how in the hell could you work deals like that? So now it's morning, a few weeks later and I'm the opening manager and the only one in the tower. I'm doing the morning meeting and around 9:20 am, mid meeting, I'm told the family in the waiting area has an appointment with Alex and they've been here since 8:30am. Of course Alex was supposed to be here, he was on the opening team. I send one of his teammates out to see if they can help his customer. As they are telling the other salesperson that they are here to buy the new luxury SUV sitting in the showroom, a fleet assistant from our Fleet Department comes and puts a sold tag on it. These people had been waiting an hour and they were here to buy a car they just watched us sell while they were looking at it and waiting for Alex who was late to work and later to the appointment he had made. I'm the manager on duty and now I have customers that want a free car because of Alex. Of course the only one we have similar to this one has a 5k higher invoice and they want the deal we promised them and on the car we promised them that we just sold right in front of them. I was being put together big time. Dan needs to solely work with this guy or he has to go, is how I rightly felt at the time. I'm being held responsible for a guy that wouldn't be here if he was on my team.

Like with Mahmoud, I started to think outside the square. This specific problem of customer's cars being sold out from under them, seemed to be an almost daily complaint in our 700 car a month dealership. We had the rule that whoever agrees to numbers first gets it, so every Saturday, here we go again, a customer would say yes to a deal on a car that somebody else still thought they were negotiating on. We were never lying at this store when we said: "somebody else wants to buy this car, you better hurry up if you want it." Of course, these people would get the most angry even after being told this. At the time, we had no process to fix this at this dealership. It was a real shit show through almost every incident. We would use the notes in our manufacturer's inventory portal, as the usual solution to tag the car as mine either incoming or on the lot to be delivered. As you can imagine, Alex's car on this morning was not tagged in our manufacturer's portal.

I became obsessed again, I knew there had to be a fix because of how my desk-log had worked to fix so many other problems. I made at least a dozen separate sheets trying to figure something out. Nothing was better than the system I had already created. I gave up. I decided that no matter what, Alex's situation would happen again. I couldn't improve upon it.

I wouldn't give up even after saying I gave up and then once again I would accidentally invent the most revolutionary follow-up system, originally just trying to solve for Alex's mismanagement and lack of organization.

I had created a sheet that I was thinking about a lot more than all the other sheets I had created. This sheet would receive all the customers that had made it to the desk-log but didn't become deals. At this point in time, we were not putting any notes on the customer lines. We were just putting lines of information with a bunch of stuff you'd see on an old paper desk-log. We had nowhere to write anything unique. It had a trade-in box, a payment and down payment box, boxes for who was involved in the deal and a "did they demo?" box etc. When I first added a "notes" box, the notes were originally not for every deal. The notes would be for "gave $500 deposit, picking car up Saturday" or "we need to send this to Cap-One." I noticed a little organic communication once I added this note box. I didn't tell anybody what was going on in my head when I added it or give any instructions. The managers just started using it. The Finance Managers would, around the same time, start turning red deals back to yellow and writing notes as to why, "still need down payment" or "wife hasn't signed yet" (we will discuss this further in chapter 8). These deals would then at night be sent over to this separate sheet I had created.

As you can imagine this sheet stacked up fast. One thing that was cool, and as I noted we will discuss more in chapter 8, was that the deals the Finance Managers still needed things on, they started reverting back to yellow, this really stuck out in this mess as I scrolled. I realized this was literally a list of all our halfway done deals in the store. This wouldn't have solved the Alex problem, but I knew I was on to something here.

I got obsessed again. The most important thing I realized was that the customers in this sheet were sort of a filter of the deals we were most likely to do. I basically ended up completely ditching the fancy CRM entirely, and as the Internet Director, past making sure the leads were answered and my guys were still doing their tasks. I had a short list of the people we were most likely to do business with, this was undisputable. When my guys got somebody in from a lead, they ended up on the desk-log and then in my follow up system if they did'nt buy. Remember this was only the people that had reached a negotiation. This is the real filter. I didn't explain to anybody what I had done, because I didn't believe it myself. I thought if my hypothesis was right, every dealership is going to need this.

I had gone from sifting and sifting through a CRM, while trying to handle what gets thrown at me all day to having this short list of people that have most recently negotiated. I didn't need the fancy CRM as the Internet Director at all. In fact, what I was doing was so much more efficient that we would sell 200 cars out of the Internet Department shortly after for the first time ever. What was I doing? I was literally only following back up on customers that had come, negotiated, and left. Now I had a note on most of them. Not like CRM notes from 5 different departments in the store and old objections. Instead, we had notes on exactly why we didn't make the deal just recently. My guys would write as the customer was leaving or right after, "credit sucks" (I told them to change that note to "Turndown" of course). Before, just the payment notes the other managers and myself would put were enough for me to plug in the numbers and look at the deal they wanted before calling them. Now I had my guys writing "wife tells him what to do." "Hey guys just write 'needs to talk to wife,' please not 'wife tells him what to do." These notes however were gold for me. They weren't textbook long explanations of what took place. They were the basics to the equation of making each deal; "wife", "trade value." I started to notice a pattern I should've already known once again on my own and that was every objection falls under a certain umbrella of about 8. I made a column with a drop down I would later open up that said "Objection", even though we can group them all. This column is for the brief sum up of the main objection. You can use it for whatever you want because we leave it open but it's usually "TD" for turndown, "payment", "down", "shopping", "unrealistic", "wife", "husband", and that's about it. These were the ONLY people I would call for months as the Internet Director and my guys would each sell 35+ cars and fast. We were doing so well because I was getting their customers back and fast. I wasn't spending time calling anybody from 3 weeks ago, unless they were in my sheet and had been there a while and hadn't picked up. I realized the extremely drastic and fast improvement had to do with of course my phone skills, but more seriously because I was only touching the people that were most "Hot." I wasn't sitting on the phone for 20 minutes with somebody the CRM told me to call from 6 months ago, who is telling me about another dealership's Service Department for 10 minutes, EVER, unless they got transferred to me. I had basically quit old customers. This may sound bad, but when you really think about it, where were my new customers coming from? They weren't new customers. They were the customers we were letting slip through the cracks. If internet was doing this, I knew retail was too.

It's a common theme and probably happened inside your store in the last 48 hours at most.

This is it:

Salesperson comes to the desk:

Salesperson: "Hey remember the Cohens from last Saturday?"

Busy desk guy: "Remind me."

Sales guy: "Doesn't matter; just called them, they bought from so and so 2 days ago on Monday and they were just here Saturday."

Busy Desk guy: "That sucks, did you follow up with them in your CRM?"

Sales guy: "I did all my tasks like I always do, did you call them?"

Desk guy: "Not sure."

Sales guy: "I did, my notes are in the CRM, I did all my tasks."

Desk guy: "I don't know what to tell you."

This is probably happening in your store right now and everyday. This is causing more problems than just lost deals. It's causing low morale of your salespeople and lowered self confidence in your management. This stopped happening in my Internet Department when I stopped using the CRM and solely followed-up using my separate sheet on my guys' customers that were most recently here. It went from a regular daily occasion of me feeling like I let my guys down and still having to point the finger at them to that literally never happening.

My guys were basically never pointing the finger at me because they let one of their deals slip through the cracks. All I was doing was calling a very short list of people all day. It was mostly the write-ups from the past 3 days and almost nobody who wasn't here within the last 2 weeks, unless still in open communication working a deal. The Hot Sheet was the only thing I used to make my calls. My guys would use the CRM for tasks. The CRM has so many people in it, that I would usually call a dozen of these people at most when using it for follow-up and then dozens more people from months ago or even years ago. The follow-up system inside the fancy CRM had me touching the customers ready to buy a lot less and wasting my time on calls with people that were not buyers right now. I'm not saying don't follow-up with old customers. We would still send out mass marketing emails to our list. If you've heard about the 80/20 rule however, it applies here in that the heavy, heavy majority of your follow-up should be towards these people that are in the market and hot right now. It seems our industry talks a lot about this but there aren't many well organized solutions. I wasn't really on to something our industry didn't know already. I just didn't solve it coming at it from that angle. What I would come to find out is that it isn't an 80/20 rule when it comes to follow-up. The rule is that the people that got to a negotiation and were just inside our showroom are around 95-98% more likely to buy than any other customer information you can pull out of your CRM. This isn't complex to understand, once again I didn't even arrive here with this information. I arrived here organically because I realized the CRM companies really didn't know what we thought they did. I wasn't a computer guy at all. I just knew what I needed to get done, I didn't stop trying getting to get it done, and the CRM just wasn't the best hammer I could find.

The Hot Sheet, according to one of my favorite dealers' testimonials in their own words "was a complete game changer" once I showed retail. Of course they were like "stop man," "stop trying to fix what isn't broken," "dude you aren't going to make it more awesome, it's already amazing," etc. Now when I decided to share I hadn't used the CRM to follow up in months, heads turned and I started a repeat shit storm.

There are a million analogies. If I give you something that works better than the thing you just bought, are you going to fight to keep using the thing that doesn't work as well? No, right? I hope not.

I come in to work the day after telling my GSM and the other managers that I wasn't using the CRM for basically anything anymore, even though my guys were obviously still using it for answering the leads and completing their tasks. I had quit the fancy CRM all together, completely. I had also gotten a department that when I started was selling 80-100 cars up past 200 cars for 3 months in a row in a matter of almost a year. I still only had 6 salespeople. I had also helped retail year over year grow over 35% in their sales. Of course I wasn't getting any credit for this and even though my desk-log was up on every computer and phone in the dealership, including my GM's, none of the credit for the massive increases, in not just sales but efficiency, productivity and overall morale, had been given to me. I was still the youngest Sales Manager in this dealership and I was still seen as somebody challenging the system, that was going to fuck up and be proven wrong eventually. I'm not complaining, just painting the real picture of what it was like. I was just trying to help and I had kept on making this desk-log better and better.

Ever since the day I thought it was my last, about a year prior to this day, that feeling hadn't returned, but it was back. I cared more about making my desk-log better than my job I realized. The dealership was my testing ground now, so I was going to test it here or somewhere else, it didn't matter to me, so when I was pulled in that's exactly what I told my GM.

Me: "Spare me."

My GM: "What?"

Me: "If this is my last day, I'm ok with that, and I even hope you guys keep using the system I created, but if you are going to make me work out of the CRM or get mad at me for selling 200+ cars the last 3 months in a row, because I did something more efficient than the CRM provides, that's fine, we can part ways."

My favorite part was hitting him with the "part ways." I think that may have done it too. In his head he probably said: "oh really, you think you're gonna part ways with me huh?, I don't think so!" That's exactly the thought his next words seemed connected to. "OK, I want to see what you did now." As soon as I showed him the yellow deals in the separate doc were all the store's halfway done deals. He got sidetracked and started asking me about the actual deals immediately. "This one just says "$500 down payment," when are they coming in? "Can I see this on mine." I show him it's the only other tab there now. I had been building out other tabs to come up with it so nobody was looking at the other sheets. I only had this one now. This is all I was interested in pursuing from the other dozen experiments I had tried. He got it instantly and actually complimented it immediately. "Yeah you are right I wouldn't know where to go to find this in the CRM." My intentions were never to set out and prove the CRM companies wrong, though that is what people assume when they hear me speak, because I do say, "I always hated the CRM's." I just hated using computers, I was never trying to prove the CRM companies didn't know what they were doing. I was only trying to solve problems. I think now, if I had been the one, or if my compensation had been tied to the money actually paying for the CRM, maybe I would've felt like my GM and felt like what I was doing was a threat to the money I was spending. Ever since Anaj showed me Google Docs, I had been trying to solve problems with this desk-log that had now evolved to a completely separate follow-up system.

What my GM would do would piss me off in the moment but later I would actually agree with his rationale and the process we would form around both my desklog and the CRM. He called a management meeting and it was all about what we were now calling "The Hot Sheet." After I had left his office that day of course, all the other managers wanted to know what happened. I just told them that I explained it to him and he got it. I didn't tell them I basically walked in and quit and he put me back together. That actually pissed them off, they all thought I was his new sidekick. This GM never played favorites though, so that was all imagination. I was actually always in the hottest water with the most amount of light shined on what I was doing and the drama that had ensued around me, building this thing over the last year. They didn't see it that way. They were all jealous, nervous and worried. Good. I still loved helping them all use my newest addition to my system. They did all give me compliments for this one saying I just revolutionized follow-up. I don't think it still made sense to any of us what I had changed. What would soon happen would be incredible. At first our GM would tell us all in this next meeting that we were all to use both systems for follow-up. The CRM and mine, which just sounds bad to begin with when hearing it. It doesn't sound like a solution at all to add more work, which is what 2 systems sounds like. I was emotional and pissed off, they still didn't get it. The other managers are making jokes "Thanks Phil!" etc. They were not really seriously mad at me, but I was mad, and I really shouldn't have been. I would come to find out. It would take maybe about a week until every other manager was saying "I'm just having my guys do their tasks in the CRM and I stay in "The Hot Sheet" all day. The metrics we would soon be able to gauge were insane. We were able to predict with astonishing accuracy, like never before, how many we would sell, to who and who was going to be selling what, etc.

Once again... organic. I started to realize that if I had been sitting in a lab as a computer developer trying to solve problems, I don't know exist, I would never be arriving at these discoveries. Most of the changes I made were purely by accident, being able to modify it as I went, and more importantly as we used it. This was amazing. This was controlled by us, not automated tasks in a non-sequential disordered way, spitting commands at you like you're a robot and the computer is the salesman. This was what we should've done to begin with for follow-up. I quickly remembered back to my days as a closer after my first 2 years in finance. I was a closer for about a year before the CRM became mainstream and we got one. I would pull out all my old 4 squares and flip through them making phone calls. I had no idea, but back then, I was calling only recent step 5's. If my customer was too old before the CRM, they got lost or simply thrown in the shred box. This is what we knew the CRM fixed when it came. It gave us the ability to amass a database and send targeted emails to these customers based on model, etc. It seemed more organized to follow up with a much larger list, but I was now realizing because of the efficiency and the effectiveness that my follow-up system had provided, it really just created chaos.

I got more obsessed. I decided that each manager should have their sheets separate because we essentially had a combo of all of our Hot Sheets. Now something I haven't even discussed also happened organically with the Hot Sheet, and that was teamwork. We could all see what we were working on. So, if I just used a finance promotion on a customer and I know it's new, and I saw Dan's customer in the Hot Sheet deal on that model, I would ask Dan, "Hey did you use the so and so certificate?" The salespeople were helping each other too. My team had started treating our deals like a shared pot for months, getting each of them to 35 units a piece one month, and all sharing 1st place. Now I'm not pitching communist ideas, quite the opposite. I actually firmly believe in giving the guy at the top of the leaderboard all the cheese. By my best guestimations, he's currently the most on point. What I'm talking about, is a team effort towards a common goal that happens organically, because we all do need a day off. The competition gets more fierce but the back watching and helping hands multiply too, which seems counterintuitive, but it isn't if you think about it. The commonality here is you have 10 people in your Hot Sheet, you start to realize that this Hot Sheet really is hot, and cools quick. These people are the people you lose when you take a day off. Guys will organically team up and call each other's Hot Sheet deals only on the other's day off. They realize they can't let these sit, that's how incredible this process truly is. Now they help each other with objections. "He said he'll call you tomorrow, he's not buying today, don't worry." When I saw this, I was stunned. The Hot Sheet had organically created a team effort to help, learn from each other, and train each other.

The Hot Sheet was now divided into sections. I had started by putting all the "yellows", the deals where we had a deposit or something signed, we called them "halfway done deals" at the top, we now call these "Step 8's." I had also separated the rest of them and grouped them by Sales Manager, so we each had a section "Phil," "David," etc. Every morning we would just take the write-ups that didn't become deals yesterday and move them to whoever's section they belonged to. The Hot Sheet itself started to become a lot of work to just maintain, but it was still beyond worth it. We didn't complain. This was helping us be so much more efficient and sell a lot more, so we didn't care. I would eventually, of course, solve all this by leaving Google Docs and creating a real software as you know, but that's much further down the road from this time.

At this point, what we had was incredible. If somebody called in sick or left the company, we knew what deals they were working. The salespeople were all wise to the fact that the "CRM leads" meant nothing when somebody left. It was the 3 deals in their Hot Sheet that everybody wanted. The 3 ups they had lackadaisically taken recently, that was all they had probably left for right now. Anything in their CRM's were needles in a haystack at best. You understand this fully, only after using this system. It's clear that the CRM is a giant list that keeps growing and growing. Your Hot Sheet has deals that are like little hourglass timers in it, they'll become what's in the CRM if you don't get on them now. If you get on them now, you are likely to make last stitch deals and pull customers out of other showrooms a lot more regularly. See, when that happens now, if your dealership isn't using a Hot Sheet, I can guarantee that the salesperson consistently doing this, has his or her own version of a Hot Sheet. It's in their pocket, on a notepad or in their iPhone notes. He or she is also aggressively working and on top of all his or her deals. This same salesperson, just like every human, doesn't operate at 100% all the time. There will be a time this salesperson isn't on top of all his or her customers or as hungry as he or she once was. Also 90% of your staff isn't this salesperson at any given time. That's why this is so huge. You now have a view of that pocket pad or phone notes, or actually a filter of what those notes should be. As if all your salespeople are aggressively on top of everything at all times. This becomes automatic, just by logging all your step 5's. Now your entire sales and management team sees everybody's Hot Sheet at all times, and it's constantly changing as you sit new customers down and the day passes. If you have a guy that calls in late or sick, it's the first thing you look at now. Its 10 lines of people that were just here if the salesperson is a 20-car guy. It's 10 phone calls to customers you also know are more likely to buy than 95-98% of the people in their CRM because these customers were just here looking at numbers. If the guy isn't working or a large producer, he may have 2 people in there. The 300 people in the CRM we use to be worried about are just like anybody else in your CRM. Some will rise from the dead, most won't. You were going to drop those on a guy too busy to work them anyway, and then get mad he didn't when they aren't really worth anything more than any random allotment of leads in your CRM. The 2 people in The Hot Sheet are all you should be worried about. You'll know this when you start using the process. It becomes clear very fast.

The best way to use the Hot Sheet Follow-Up System is of course by also utilizing or implementing the Product Specialist System. Your Product Specialists will have no access to The Daily Desk or The Hot Sheet. On the flip side, your management team, including your closers, will barely use the CRM outside of making sure the Product Specialist's are. They will live inside the Hot Sheet. They will always have plenty of calls to make and they're literally not just the cream at the top of the coffee, they are the tiny sprinkles on top of the bubbles only. Soon we would go from doing new car walkarounds and walking the used car lot in our meetings to doing solely what would first be called "Hot Sheet" meetings. Today, this is a Save-A-Deal Meeting or a Make-A-Deal Meeting, which of course existed way before my desk-log.

You really aren't having an effective meeting without some type of a Hot Sheet.

You do not need to be utilizing the Product Specialist System for this to be effective, it just makes it better. If you do not use Product Specialists, have your desk work the Hot Sheet and let your salespeople work the CRM. Let me or somebody else at Central Desking spend an hour with your team and it will be on like Donkey Kong!

THE BRAIN IN COLORADO

We were in our usual meeting, doing walkarounds, standing by our big glass wall that lines the street the dealership sits on. This was a "landlocked" store. We had parking lots all over the city to store cars. We could only fit about 12 cars in the showroom, and we sold 700+ per month out of this building. There was a regular sized sidewalk and then a major road. We heard a rumble coming towards us and loud, we all turn and look and see a truck about to drive right through the glass into the showroom. As you can imagine we all dart different ways and towards the back wall away from the inevitable when we noticed it. Expletives are flying and then BOOM!, the truck comes crashing into the showroom and out comes a late twenties, obviously intoxicated, shirtless and shoeless driver that immediately went towards a new showroom car and got in it and tried looking for a key he would later tell us " to drive back out the other window." I was on the other side of the showroom, but a couple guys who were close pulled him out off the car and held him down. The cops would come, and he would get arrested. The following day however, our windows were boarded up and they were prepping new glass etc. between the small sidewalk we had and inside the showroom, so we took our morning meeting into a finance office.

Immediately as we get back there, because we usually did walk-arounds, we didn't really know what we were going to do and Dave goes, "I have an idea. At my old dealership we used to do Save-A-Deal Meetings. It was a pain in the ass but your system actually does what we used to try to do that was a huge pain in the ass; we use to have to print out all the deal screens we worked the prior day." I'm was stunned at the time, wanting to know more (I foolishly thought I had invented everything we were doing around my system), but Dave jumps in to put the desk-log on the Finance Manager's big screen in his office and starts to head up the meeting. He says "Ok, all the deals we worked are right here." He goes to yesterday's tab, he starts at the top and 1 by 1 we all talked about the deal after he would ask the salesperson "tell me what happened?" I had been in the business for 12 years and this was my first what I like to now call "Make A Deal Meeting", and it would've never happened, had a drunk driver not crashed into our showroom the prior day.

We weren't doing what most call "Save A Deal Meetings" before and I'd later like the term "Make A Deal Meetings." We would walk the used car lot and do walk arounds with the salespeople. Remember this store didn't have closers. We as Sales Managers would be pushed to close deals and this is pretty standard industry advice, but what happens, is you get stuck with a customer while others wait. It's not a sustainable and efficient process and the only reason you have people putting up with it, is because it's a standard expectation now. You need a guy behind the computer and a guy on the floor when you think about it critically. I'm not sure why we have top performing and well known dealerships operating this way. It's completely counterintuitive. This places unreasonable expectations that don't help your guys do what unreasonable expectations can sometimes do in other places; make people better. There is no solving for taking the toll booth operator out of the booth and the line piling up, sorry. Closer's or Assistant Sales Managers are the solve for this, and on the flip side I do recommend a T.O. from your Desk Managers after your ASM is stuck. This is a far cry from expecting your desk guys to work the desk and close all their deals from the 1st pencil. I know some stores are very successful in operating this way, that doesn't mean it's not holding you back. I assure you it is. There's well-oiled and then there's organized chaos. I know how most of the Los Angeles dealerships operate and they are the latter. Well known stores, you'd think are better than yours, are sometimes just in the right place in the right market doing a couple things really well. Fleet Departments and turning used cars quickly over the internet are 2 common examples of wild success in stores with no processes. Now imagine if these stores did add these processes.

If the desk-log I had made was "Sales Crack", the Make-A-Deal Meeting was the sales crack pipe. We began to gather daily and talk about what we now call "yesterday's step 5's." We would briefly take a look at the Hot-Sheets and call it a day. Oh boy, you know there was another spit yell session too, when our GM found out we had just randomly changed our entire meeting process he had setup. Fortunately, I wasn't even there, my GSM told me about it, and he got the spit. About time!

He also somehow convinced him that these meetings were a lot more productive and more important and got the walk-arounds reduced to Saturday's. Now I do recommend a Training Director for your Product Specialists that does walk-arounds and product training while your Closers/ASM's, whatever you want to call them, sit in your Make-A-Deal Meetings with management every morning. I also recommend that if you are the GM or the owner, that you go to these meetings as often as you possibly can. You'll probably make a deal yourself. You'll be able to give ideas and more importantly, you'll know a lot about what is going on right now in your dealership. There is always a disconnect of information. If you aren't in the trenches, what you know cannot help your team nearly as much as a real world example of you helping them make a real deal. This is such an amazingly easy way to know so much about your staff and store and with a small allotment of time. It's no surprise that a dealer group with 20+ stores from Florida to California, attend these meeting as owners in all of their stores. Not everyday, obviously. Approximately once a month per store. They also mandate their GM's are present. By holding a daily meeting, you have the ability to quickly manage situations as they arise. Mainly, you'll know exactly how on the market each one of your closers is everyday first thing in the morning. You will also know exactly what deals they are working after this meeting. The organic teamwork towards a common goal we had created just using my desk-log was again 10x'ed by these meetings.

When we stopped doing walk-arounds first thing in the morning and instead did these meetings, we started the day focused on making deals. This is a massive shift in culture. The culture had previously been "who was good at walk-arounds today and who sucks so bad they probably won't be able to sell cars" to "what deals are we making today and how can we all help each other make our deals?" Pretty simple.

(Note: Walk-arounds or product training and these meetings are both important. The only organized solve for both is having Product Specialists and ASM's.)

The most important steps to implementing these meetings are:

1.) Consistency in holding the meetings, Everyday.

2.) Consistency of objective, structure, and why the meeting is taking place. If you just hold morning meetings, they can quickly turn into what the most recent frustrations are, and with what or who. When this happens, you're now just holding a nagging session. I did not allow this in my meetings. If anybody starts complaining about a person who isn't there, I would just say "come tell me about it after the meeting." This isn't a place to bring down morale and divert focus. This is the place to get laser focused on making deals, to do this you have to be tracking your Step-5's.

"FACE...OFF..."

"If you can't bump this guy 5 fucking dollars Cheatham, I'm gonna turn your ass..."

-Jay, 2007

Throughout my career up to this point I had been subpoenaed a few times and never actually had to go to court. I had had a couple other investigators involved in different issues I had been a part of, never anything I did of course! But this phone call was frightening. I had a voicemail from a reporter at a local TV station. At first I thought it was a joke. It wasn't. It was real. A customer had called the station and told them we ran her credit to 11 or so banks and she never signed a credit application with us, because she didn't like her experience. Why is he calling me? I think. This cannot be my customer as he tells me this story. It didn't sound like anybody that worked in our store. She was saying that she filled out a credit app then changed her mind and a "blonde-haired boy" ran her credit to "all the banks" anyway. I get her name, look her up, log into our online banking portal and we had shot-gunned her to every bank. I take the newsman's number and tell him I'll look into it. I knew which Finance Manager had submitted her because his initials were on the submission. I went to my GSM. I told him what was going on and of course he has me retell it to our GM. He tells me "You're the only blonde-haired boy" even though I don't have blonde hair. Nobody did either so I was "the boy." He calls the Finance Manager in and the Finance Manager said he didn't submit it. He went on to say that all the Desk Managers have his banking portal login, which you already know caused more problems not addressing the newsman about to run a story. And he has my name, great! She

94

wasn't on my desk-log, and of course was never logged into a CRM, and we didn't even have the credit app used to submit the deal. We would end up writing this lady a check for $5,000, I found out later, just to go away. We never knew who she dealt with or exactly what had happened. I have my suspicions of who it was but that's it. As a result my desk-log was utilized for an entirely new process I had already been doing.

I was the only one using the T.O. column I had put on my desk-log. I used it because I know my short term memory isn't that great when it comes to remembering people. I learned this weird fact I would've never learned if I hadn't been in some sort of volume customer service role. If you bought a car from me a week ago and came in a week later, I remembered you perfectly. If you came in yesterday and came back the next day, I wouldn't remember you at all. This scared me a little bit. I would find out it's pretty normal with a high volume of customers and hand shaking with a lot of different people. It still bothered me and I hated it when it would happen. So, anytime I met somebody, they were obviously already on my desk-log, so I would put my initials in the T.O. column and that's all that meant. Nobody else was using it. I probably greeted 30% of the customers throughout the process. Mostly the ones that would buy, so I didn't have my initials on too many, about 20%, but I would always put them there if I met the customer.

The question of course from our GM was "how do we not know who dealt with this lady when we are basically using 2 CRMS!" All eyes point at me of course and that line was pretty funny and true.

I of course spoke up and said I had been using the T.O. column and told them why. Not sure if it will help but that's what I do. It was immediately mandated, followed with an "All your initials should be in every column," which I disagree with and doesn't make any sense. He meant we should be touching every customer and closing our deals. We did a lot, but it just doesn't make efficient sense when I can close a decent deal from the desk and only go talk to the people I need to, it just doesn't, guys.

So we all start putting our initials. This was now micromanaged. Our GM was able to directly ask in any Make-A-Deal meeting that he would walk into "we had 10 total write-ups yesterday and you didn't T.O. that guy to another manager?", and by briefly glancing at the desk-log. I had made our GM's job a lot easier. I had messed up because the other 3 managers thought it was all my fault. He could now manage them much more effectively and ask poignant questions they sometimes had no answers for, with just the addition of this column. He was able to manage his customers being second faced. Also with all the salespeople or your ASM's looking at this, they won't usually allow their Sales Manager to lie and say they touched their customers when they didn't.

SYSTEMS CHECK

"Can you put the staple here and not here the next time you staple the CarFax?"

-Procrastinating Finance Manager at the sales desk as the customer waits, for finance.

"**W**hat the fuck man, my people have to go, these finance people are so slow!" This was George with a deal in his hands running back and forth in front of the finance offices cursing while all the managers had customers in their offices on a busy Saturday. This was normal behavior. He thought every Finance Manager was Mahmoud. I know because I briefly worked in finance while he was on the desk. I wowed the guy 10 times in a row, he still expected me to fuck up his deal. He was the only one. I guess he was traumatized from working with Mahmoud for 50 something years. If so, I understand and forgive him. Other than these tantrums and melt downs over F+I, George had it together and was a great guy. "George is flipping out in finance again bud, go try and calm him down," David tells me. I go back there and he gets worse "you don't understand 'Cheats' he called me, I've been dealing with this for decades." "Ok George, well let's go curse away from the customers about it."

We had already fixed the finance end of finance rotation with my desk-log, so I started staying up all night thinking again. For this I didn't even know what I was thinking about, I just had so much confidence in being able to figure out how to solve problems with my desk-log, I thought I could get it to do something,

I had no idea what though. I started tinkering again. I thought there was some sort of rotation log I could add. I played with another couple dozen sheets for no reason, they were all total flops nobody wanted to use. Finally, I realized I couldn't solve the George problem with my desk-log. The George problem was absolutely a process problem but not one solved by an addition to my desk-log. Once I started thinking away from the desk-log, I would figure it out and it would all come back to the desk-log. I just wouldn't need to add anything. Now the process I'm about to go over, once again organically discovered is practiced at most Harley dealerships already, before I ever came up my own version, with just a Service Department a half mile down the street.

I remembered back to my first dealership, where the Product Specialists would go over the car or take the customers to service when finance was busy. That dealership now actually makes the Product Specialists show the Service Department during the demo. They have a time stamp on their guest card, and visit the Service Department before they turn it into the desk.

I pitched it to our GM. I walked right in and without bringing up George, I told him what my old dealership use to do and said, "when a customer signs, why don't we have the salesperson drive them over to service and meet a service writer and look at our Service Department?" We did our deliveries in a back alley that fit very few cars, so when we had a lot of deliveries the salespeople would actually drive the car off the property, park it, and do their delivery. Our Service Department was the perfect idea. I know my GM had responded before to every "at my last dealership" statements from every person he ever heard it from with "well, why aren't you at your last dealership then?" I was brazen to approach it this way. Maybe he was thinking about his service retention, maybe he was just tired of dealing with me but he just said, "great idea get it going."

We started doing it the next day, it was as simple "as when

PHILIP J. CHEATHAM

you're deal goes to finance, you have to take your customer to service now." They all started listening, but I did my part to go around to everybody and explain why, so they knew it was for them to relieve customer anxiety, etc when waiting for finance. Of course this new process created a problem instantly that nobody would think about beforehand. Now the Finance Managers were complaining that they couldn't interview their customers because they were over in service after closing for an hour.

Simple fix and this took zero nights lying awake. Ok, once we close them you come interview them, then they'll take them to service. Done. Simple. Finally.

It was amazing. George was no longer worried (most of the time unless he had Mahmoud until Mahmoud left). Once Mahmoud left I don't think I ever saw another George meltdown. He still was whining and bitching about the Finance Managers, but he was never again given the situation to full on melt down and forget where he was.

There is a ton of opportunity is this process outside of alleviating the dreaded finance wait. Sometimes I know it's harder on us than the customer. The reason Harley does it is they sell motor clothes and parts on what is usually called a "family tour." Once they close the deal, they go around to all the departments after their finance interview and are told to make "wish lists" at the really organized stores. When they get to finance, the Finance Manager can add these wish lists into their loans if there is room. I know most franchise car brands don't sell too many accessories. I also know of luxury stores in South Florida that sell cars you wouldn't think would be accessorized and then lead the customer into a room with chrome wheels etc., to upsell the same way. There is a ton of opportunity here. The first thing usually on a dealer's mind is their service retention. This is a great way to make sure your customers come back to your Service Department for their service, especially if you're in a big city with a lot

99

of other options.

We had a horrid service return rate of 29%, because our Service Department was down the street in another building and there are other dealerships with much nicer Service Departments in this city. We were solving for a totally unrelated issue, but because the salespeople started taking their customers and introducing them to a Service Manager while waiting for finance, this same dealership now has a 60% return service rate, which is great for where this dealership is located.

Finance sells more because they never have a customer standing in front of their office being told by their salesperson "it's that guy doing your paperwork." This needs a big note: I have 5 years of finance experience in volume stores and this is the best thing you can do to guarantee you don't add backend to a deal. Most of your Finance Managers don't know how to raise this issue and it's happening. You are not protecting your customers that would buy protection and you are leaving money all over the table if your Sales Department is doing this to your F+I. It's pretty simple. "That's the reason you're waiting sir," "that" is now going to sell you thousands of dollar's worth of F+I products? "That" could be really good, their chances of putting a great deal together, if there was one just plummeted like Enron stock in 3 seconds out of a brief anxiety held by your salesperson, not even the customer most of the time. We can't blame the people if we don't put the processes in place. We will get what we tolerate. Service walks are a no-brainer. If you have accessories to upsell, even better, take them there too. They just said yes to the vehicle, they are in buying mode, don't ruin it! Capatalize on it!

TSUNAMI

"What if you did that with all your customers?"

-Mahmoud, 2015

I'm taking a very unusual break in front. I'm sitting in chairs the salespeople sit in and aren't supposed to for maybe the 3rd time in the year and a half. It's a weird Saturday around 3pm. You'd think the Super Bowl was going on. I had called our entire Hot-Sheet 5 or 6 times, had appointments, but just nothing going on for the first minute in 6 months, you know what I'm talking about. An unusual rest seemingly provided for by the heavens, if just for a moment to take in my surroundings.

I'm sitting here for about 90 seconds when I hear from the other end of the showroom "your Used Car Manager is a thief! What an asshole!" You then hear a chair move fast and some shuffling and then "were leaving! where's our car?" We had valet, so I tell the receptionist who I was sitting next to, "call over to valet and tell them they have this guy coming, I'm going to go get his name." I walk over to the other Sales Managers and try and ask what's going on. I'm told "it was a first pencil, the guy just lost it." As we are having this conversation, we hear a big smash and everybody runs to the back. The customer had found his own car and key and literally drove it through 2 other cars to get it out where it was parked and smashed up his car and 2 others. He kept going and went home. Knowing he would be arrested immediately if we called the police, we said "let's give the guy a chance first and give him a call." Now that he wasn't in our store, we were actually having a little fun anticipating this conversation as you can imagine. "Why don't you call him Phil?" "You weren't involved." "Why Not?" David: "Hey Phil what do I put in those notes?" Like I'm the note controller. I just say "give me the guy's number and I'll call him." "Hello is this Stephen?" "Yeah, who's this?" "This is Philip, just calling with the customer Service Department over here at so and so dealership, just calling to make sure my team was kind and curious, how was your visit today?" I press mute to try to stop laughing. "Well you sound nice, but your Used Car Manager is a piece of shit!" "I'm sorry about that, were you able to leave in a car today?" Mute again, now we are laughing our asses off. "Yeah! Mine! You people don't want to do business with me down there, I tried." "Well let me look up what is going on, would that be ok if I look into your deal and see what happened? What were you trying to get for your trade? I'm assuming that was the issue?" "Alright I have a 2009 Cadillac STS with... And KBB says it's worth $12,000 on the low end and you people offered me $1,100 so I got out of there, that's thievery!" "That doesn't sound right can I put you on hold?" "What were you giving this guy for his trade?" "$11,000" "Are you serious?" David: "Why?" "He thinks we offered him $1,100." David: "Oh shit, Oh fuck." "Hello, sir, are you there? So I just called down to the Sales Department, just so you know, they were offering you $11,000 and they said you got extremely upset and left in a hurry, even damaging some of our vehicles on your way out, is that true?" "If that's true, I messed up big and I apologize, can you find out if I can pay for the vehicle damage? Did you guys already file a report?" "I'll find out sir, hold on." I left him on the line for a good 15 minutes and I did that so that he would be appreciative when I got back on the line and gave him the good news that we didn't call the police on him. I kept looking at the phone to see if there was still a call and he was still there, after what I felt was enough stewing, I picked the phone back up. We all got our kicks out of it. The guy was well off and would come back and not only do the deal with the $11,000 for his trade but he would write us a personal check later that we would be nice about and charge internal pricing to fix the 2 cars he wedged his between to leave the dealership.

We were laughing about the whole thing of course a few days later and how crazy it was. Mahmoud happened to be there and heard about it for the first time. I don't think anybody told Mahmoud anything, ever. He may have missed the truck crash through the showroom and just thought the glass broke. It's totally possible.

So Mahmoud is blown away hearing this "When did this happen? Wow, and you got him back to buy? Your system is pretty cool. You know you could call all the customers that leave and find out what they say, saying the same stuff you said to that guy." Everybody starts laughing. "Yeah Mahmoud, we aren't in finance, we have to follow up with everybody, that's not a new thing." Mahmoud says "No, I mean like 5 minutes like you did, after they leave." "It was like 15, he was already home." "OK, 15 minutes, you call and ask what you asked." David cuts in, "Yeah, Phil asked the guy "how was your visit" after the guy just took out 2 fucking cars." Mahmoud says "and he came back and bought a car!" Just like that, exact quote, because I would hear it over and over again all night pondering this call idea. Of course I would later find out this was also already a thing; it was called a U-Turn call and tons of dealers do them, but a small fraction of overall dealerships actually make this call.

I told myself I would test it and I was able to sleep. I went in the next day and told my team, "Hey when you let somebody go, always write a note." (I advise your Desk Managers write these notes, we had not fine-tuned these processes.) You want the person ultimately in charge of the deal leaving the note, as to why they couldn't make a deal and let the customer go. It is most important to write the note as they go, while it's still fresh. Of course I thought I needed to create another doc again and played with another half-dozen, ultimately realizing I didn't need to change my desk-log at all to execute this process on every step 5 that left. Here are some numbers so you can understand the call volume here. I consistently had around a 50% closing ratio with everything I was already doing and I was selling 200 cars. You can do the math; for me in a department selling 200 cars, this was 200 calls a month. The floor was a little lighter than me on their closing ratios, around 35% average. They each sold 100 deals, so for them they would also be making around 200 calls.

Most days I would only make 5 or 6 calls. I'd sell 5 or 6 write-ups on an average day Mon-Fri and I'd walk 5 or 6 write-ups. I was only calling the ones I walked. At first I called them all. I immediately noticed I really couldn't make the same call I made that day to people I had met, it just didn't work the same. What was working was the calls to people I hadn't met, and immediately. I didn't turn anybody around for the first few days, but I kept making the calls. They were valuable because I established a connection I thought. I was also writing notes on what they told me, usually consistent with the notes we wrote when they left. Sometimes I would get extra info we didn't have or know about, so I kept making them.

Day 3 making calls: I call a customer that was just with one of my guys that I didn't meet. I saw him in the store and I was not hopeful at all, he looked like he was bored while he was here and wanted to go the entire time. He answers, "Hi this is Philip from so and so dealership, I saw that you made a visit into our store today and I just wanted to make sure my team was kind and courteous, how was your visit?" "Well, I came in to buy the used car you guys have online, but Sam wanted me to buy new and I can't buy new so I left." I'm in my head going, "huh?" The notes just say "thinking overnight." I said "that's too bad you went through that, I apologize. You don't happen to have the stock number to that car?" Knowing personality types, I knew he would, just throwing that in there. He says "yes its H492012" like he had it memorized. I said "yep, that car is here, I'm not sure why Sam wouldn't let you buy it, do you still want it?" "I don't know, I'm already home." I said: "You know what, come on back down and I'll have it cleaned for you before you get here and I'll get you through as a VIP so you can skip the finance line." A lie I always tell whether they wait or not, "Oh that's another VIP." I would argue this is not morally wrong in anyway, you are just making people feel special and calming their anxieties. "I'll fill up your gas tank, just come on back and let me make it up to you. My name is Philip, ask for me when you get here so I can make sure everybody knows you are VIP."

It just worked again. This one I stayed up all night thinking about. "Would we have ever gotten this guy back?" On and on questioning myself late-at-night.

I hadn't yet talked to Sam who used to joke about not selling any used all the time, so I had totally believed the customer's interpretation of events. I would talk to Sam who would tell me the guy never said anything once; I was sure Sam was lying and I went on with life.

I would continue making these calls and my guys knew I was making them, so something else happened. They would now be at the sales desk working deals with me and before they let their guy go, they would make comments I picked up on like, "You want to talk to this guy, so you make sure I didn't stop him from buying used?" I wouldn't make the calls if I had just met them and didn't have anybody else making those yet either, because they were not effective at all, I knew that. They had just told me whatever their objection was, me calling to ask again or having Sam call on his own deal was awkward, weird and it didn't work at all, like when I hadn't met them and they thought I was a 3rd party to the deal. They would spew information at me almost every time. Most of the time it was stuff we already knew, but occasionally I'd make a deal that confused me like this one.

After having a few deals similar to Sam's from these calls

over a period of a couple weeks I hadn't yet put it together, but I was starting to. Enough time had passed, and I didn't know why, but I wanted to hear from Sam about that customer again without him thinking he was in trouble. This was still the "turn-around" that stood out to me for some reason. I grabbed him and pulled him into an office. "Hey man, I don't care, I'm just trying to figure out something here. That customer from a couple weeks ago you kept trying to push him to new and he was telling the truth, right?" "Boss, I swear, he told me once in the beginning 'I only want used.' I did what we are supposed to do right? I showed him a new, he never said anything after that, I swear, he was cool with it, he didn't tell me that was the reason at all, I was shocked when you got him back in, I swear."

It would take me another month of making these calls and another dozen deals turned around, doing this process before I realized Sam wasn't lying.

Most of our customers will be on a scale from at least a little squeaky to loud when they aren't getting what they want and guide us to help them. Most customers we try and switch from used to new will tell us if it isn't happening. "Hey bud sell me the used, not buying a new" etc. We stop and sell them the used. There is another type of customer or personality type that will go along with it and never give you the real objection. What was weird, is that they would spew it over the phone at me only 15 minutes after leaving.

This took a ton of thinking, but I came up with my hypothesis that I now consider a proven theory. I thought "we are missing these customers and always have been," because they don't tell us what's wrong and by the time we usually call them in 24, 48, or 72 hours, they already got online somewhere else and are looking at another car to try again and will NEVER tell you or anybody in your staff the real reason. They will only express the frustration while still in the frustration to a 3rd party that asked before they move to coming up with a solution to move on. Once they've moved on, you will never get them back. You won't ever even find out the problem, ever. This personality type ends up in our store all the time and tells us this same story. And we get the deals because they guide us when they arrive. "I went to so and so and they would only sell me a new." We are like "cool, great, I'll sell you a used." The other dealership will never even know what the problem was. This personality type is too nice and won't do anything they think somebody else will get mad about or go against what they ask. It is the uber passive personality type. Its 5-10% of the population, depending on your brand funny enough. The only way to set up a net and catch this customer is with the U-Turn call.

Doing U-turn calls will also improve confidence. When I would call and hear exactly what Sam wrote in the notes, It confirmed we knew where we were on that deal. Sometimes I would get extra information that would help, but nothing way off, still a win. Other times, I would make deals we would've never made without making these calls. Eventually, we had the BDC (Business Development Center) make these calls for us, when a note got put in from the desk as to why a customer was leaving. They would wait 15 minutes and call. When this happened and I was talking to a customer, I even found myself pushing a little harder because I didn't want BDC to find out something I didn't. I knew exactly how it worked, but everybody else felt the same way. That is good. Everybody knew when letting their customer go, that they would get a phone-call. It made us a little nervous, but it made us deals. You feel better going home when you know you pushed for every deal you touched too. Sales notch up, again. These weren't sales calls. They are so easy, your 12-year-old can make them. People will tell you what happened before they have time to think about it and make a new plan. I learned that this is true across the board for all personality types making these calls, including me:

If I'm still frustrated,
I'll tell you why.

Once I've moved to a
new solution,...
"I'm good, everything was fine,
thanks, gotta go"... click.

We also now had 2 sets of notes for our Make-A-Deal meetings. We had the Sales Manager note as to why they left, right after they left, and the BDC note from their U-Turn call. Now in the Make-A-Deal meetings, we would either get confidence, extra info or a "wtf that's probably a deal, make that call as soon as we get out of this meeting" from the U-turn call notes.

If you are reading this and realize that this process will guarantee you extra deals, but think it's a heavy lift, I assure you this is one of the easiest things you can ever do. The exact call script I refined and use now is: "Hello my name is Philip, I see you made a visit to our dealership today, I just wanted to make sure my team was kind and courteous and you had a great visit." Let them talk until they stop. Then ask: "Did you get in a new vehicle today?" Play naive and let them talk again. This does not take a salesperson as you will do no closing on this call. You want to end the call with, "I will forward this information on and hopefully we can get you in a new vehicle."

The easiest way is to just log all your write-ups on the Daily Desk.

Once you let your customer go, put a note about why they left. Have somebody else watching the screen that you never need to refresh and make these calls as your customers leave. If you have a BDC Department, this is a great task for them as they will watch the Daily Desk in your store organically for many other reasons.

A SUNRISE IN THE MIDDLE
OF THE PACIFIC

"I can't close a thing today, what about you?"

-David with 9 out, before my desk-log

One thing that completely halted at the advent of using my desk-log was us constantly packing each other and fucking with each other at the desk. I can't describe this change and how drastic it was and how none of us even talked about it for a while.

"Hey Dave, remember when you used to tell me you had the worst day and had me convinced, then I'd come in the next day and you sold 12?" (laughs) "Hahaha yeah that was great, so much fun, can't do that anymore because of your desk-log." But the truth is we used to all do it to each other. If you aren't at your sales desk and you have bunch of guys, it's happening. It was fun. It's not a huge deal, we could handle it and it was fun and funny and we all missed it a little.

David was legitimately not mad because we also all helped each other now. Because we could all see each other's deals working live. When somebody on your team had a write-up, it went on my desk-log. We all saw it. We also saw the customer name, model, stock number, and salesperson and if they were good to send to finance or if we need help after running their credit. "Dan you got 3 declines over there?" "Let me send those to Cap-One for you, my guys are all test driving." "Phil, you're working a FRD760? You know those just got more cash today?" "Damn Phil, you are killing us, more deals than all of us added up!" No sandbagging, I couldn't get away with it now either, I used to do it back to David. We never knew what the other had. We'd have our teams silent too, this is normal. My desk-log had eliminated this and actually made things much more fun and more productive.

Our GM would eventually give access to the owner, who would keep it up and watch the deals being worked in real-time from home.

TICK TOCK, TICK TOCK

"The future belongs to those who prepare for it."

-Jim Moran

O ne of my favorite sayings, that I believe is most pertinent for the necessary preparation we all need to survive the world's current uncertainty is:

"There is no such thing as being on time, you will only be early or too late."

If this is true, which it is, looking at where to live, how to do business and how to handle things like the "new normal" going forward, we must anticipate or we will be forced to react, and then we will be too late. If history repeats itself, most of us will be too late. Most of us will be forced to react after ignoring the signs given to us, to anticipate and make the changes necessary to survive and thrive. The silver lining is the same as it's always been, those who anticipate what's coming will come out on the other side of this with larger market shares and better businesses. Every economic downturn in our lifetimes and centuries before, have been massive transfers of wealth. Unfortunately, those who ignore the signs given, and hope for things to return to normal without adjusting as these signs are given, will be the ones who transfer what they have to those who did prepare and didn't ignore the signs to change now. This is going to be true concerning our businesses, our investments and even where we live and where we send our children to school. We must strategize by analyzing future scenarios. We must analyze by looking at what is happening, not what we want, or hope will happen. The world will not have moved against you. You will have already made the decision to move against the world.

-The Silver Lining-

The scariest times for most of us, have always been the greatest opportunities for those willing to move against the herd. The world's most valuable companies were pretty much all started in economic downturns. Grant Cardone talks about this a lot. He says: "expand when everybody else is contracting." He's not alone in attributing his massive success to this ability. The phone you have in your pocket and the app you buy things with on that phone are also the results of this ability. It is an ability. It's an ability that the masses cannot comprehend, let alone act upon. It takes an instinctual confidence and knowledge outside of common understandings, for one to stand against the many. This is what you must do to win. If you don't prepare to win big now, the best you will do is survive. Surviving sucks, let's be honest. Those that just survive will also suffer huge losses. Those that live it to the limit, will see massive gains and massive success. It won't be your fault or mine when others ignore this advice and follow the herd, contracting together. It is definitely your fault and mine, if we know this and don't act now.

"If you don't prepare to win big now, the best you will do is survive."

When I first started writing this chapter, I started writing different stories one after the other that I kept deleting. One story could not illustrate what I wanted to get across. After writing what you just read above, I decided that I would then ask you to think about your own stories of people you know, maybe even you, that fit into what I am writing about. Think about your own procrastinations you've had and the ones you see others currently having, that are clear to you and not clear to them. Hoping we will wake up to a pre-Corona Virus world is a procrastination. Hoping the inevitable asset collapses won't happen is a procrastination. Hoping our Federal and State governments will switch course on the policies they are tripling down on is a procrastination. It's procrastination in simple preparation. Playing out the very real scenarios we have upon us, is power. Being afraid is and has always been a debilitating weakness. Taking action in the face of uncertainty is always awarded ten-fold. This idea is simple, the challenge is difficult. I believe we are all always being challenged to do what is most difficult. This is where Greatness lies, it's our duty to see the signs and lift our Greatness up.

The stories I was going to tell to illustrate what I just wrote about conceptually, mostly pertained to the dealers that either didn't understand what I was offering or just don't like being first-movers. That is most of you. That is most of us. Inaction is a very normal human action. Big winners are abnormal, not normal. I just illustrated what it takes to be a first-mover. It's an ability that most of us cannot comprehend. There is a book called "Crossing the Chasm" that breaks down innovators, early adopters, early majority, late majority and laggards scientifically into a bell-curve. I highly recommend this book to everybody. It provides applicable principles to the entirety of our decision-making skills in life and business. Reading this book was very interesting and insightful for me, not just because it gave me insight into the first users of Central Desking, but it gave me insight into my own life and the decisions I've made. I'd love to say I found out I was an innovator. I found out that most of my life, I've been a laggard. Most of my life, I have not been into new technology. It scared me and more importantly frustrated me. My desk-log was actually birthed out of me being a total laggard combined with a push from my sadistic GM that put me in charge of the Internet Department. Being open to new technology still frightens me. Being an innovator, which is defined in the book "Crossing the Chasm" as somebody who is willing to use something without seeing anybody else use it, is still outside of my inherent personality and desires. Knowing all of this about myself, allowed me to make decisions like natural innovators and I'd say I've now become an innovator. I have to challenge my natural fears and hesitations constantly. Gold is always found within challenging ourselves.

Your competitors that you know, who are not natural innovator types, may have already started challenging themselves. They may have already decided to change course and act on the signs given, instead of hoping for them to just go away.

My Answer: The Time Is Now.

Philip J. Cheatham:

Podcast: www.DealerProcessSecrets.com
(also on itunes and all major platforms)

philip@centraldesking.com

Daily Desk:

www.centraldesking.com

800-801-2824

hello@centraldesking.com

https://www.facebook.com/CentralDesking/

Training Courses:

www.centraldeskinguniversity.com

Newsletter:

www.theautomotivesoftware.com

Listen to this audiobook for free@:

www.philipcheatham.com

7 FIGURE

PRODUCER
TRAINING COURSE

www.CentralDeskingUniversity.com

www.CentralDeskingUniversity.com

FREE Newsletter & Articles written by:

Philip Cheatham & More

www.theAutomotiveSoftware.com

ABOUT THE AUTHOR

Philip J. Cheatham

Philip J. Cheatham is the founder of CentralDesking.com. Philip has spent over 15 years working in some of the country's most well-known and top-performing automotive and motorcycle dealerships. His years of experience working on the front lines of the industry led him to create a revolutionary desk-log and follow-up system that only a "real car guy" could create. His transparent and direct style of teaching the fundamentals and finer points of sales processes is not only refreshing but enlightening. In these times of change, Philip and his company Central Desking have become the go-to for innovative, forward thinking, effective, cutting edge software and processes to carry dealers from surviving to thriving.

Made in United States
North Haven, CT
20 October 2021